Bernard Lowry

D0587317

Discovering
Fortifications

from the Tudors to the Cold War

Shire Publications

This book is dedicated to the many friends in whose company, over several decades, I have enjoyed the rich variety of British fortifications.

British Library Cataloguing in Publication Data: Lowry, Bernard. Discovering fortifications: from the Tudors to the Cold War. – (Discovering series; 296) 1. Fortification – Great Britain – History 2. Military architecture – Great Britain – History 3. Great Britain – History – Military I. Title 623.1'941. ISBN-13: 978 0 7478 0651 6. ISBN-10: 0 7478 0651 9.

Front cover: *St Mawes Castle in Cornwall was the most elaborately decorated of Henry VIII's artillery forts. In the Second World War it supported a coastal defence battery.*

Back cover: *Landguard Fort, Suffolk. The 1875 entrance to the new barracks and casemated front.*

ACKNOWLEDGEMENTS
The photograph on page 32 is acknowledged to the English Heritage Photo Library (photograph by Skyscan Balloon Photography). The photographs on pages 49 (bottom), 63 (top) and 104 (top) are by Cadbury Lamb. Other photographs are by the author.

Published in 2006 by Shire Publications Ltd, Cromwell House, Church Street, Princes Risborough, Buckinghamshire HP27 9AA, UK. (Website: www.shirebooks.co.uk) Copyright © 2006 by Bernard Lowry. First published 2006. Number 296 in the Discovering series. ISBN-10: 0 7478 0651 9; ISBN-13: 978 0 7478 0651 6.
Bernard Lowry is hereby identified as the author of this work in accordance with Section 77 of the Copyright, Designs and Patents Act, 1988.

Printed in Great Britain by Ashford Colour Press Ltd, Unit 600, Fareham Reach, Fareham Road, Gosport, Hampshire PO13 0FW.

Contents

1
Introduction

Different systems of fortification have developed and declined in the British Isles over the past three millennia in reaction to internal and external threats. In the prehistoric period promontory forts were built along the western coasts of the British Isles, and in upland areas hillforts were constructed, often enlarged and strengthened on a heroic scale. The arrival of the Roman legions led to the building of legionary fortresses, campaign and practice camps and, as a reaction to the hostile northern tribes, the construction of the Hadrianic and Antonine Walls. In England the native populations were either coaxed into Roman towns such as Wroxeter or driven out of their hillforts following bloody sieges. The Boudican revolt made it necessary to build walls around previously open Roman towns such as Colchester. The generally deteriorating security situation in the empire led to the provision of wall towers on which to mount artillery in existing fortresses together with the building of new forts along the Saxon Shore (the southern and eastern English coasts subject to Saxon attack). The gradual movement of Saxon people into England during the empire's decline led to the later building of fortified Saxon burghs against a new threat from the Danes, while Offa's Dyke was built in the eighth century to control Welsh incursions into Saxon Mercia.

In the eleventh century a small number of Norman knights were invited by Edward the Confessor to settle in England, and it is believed that they were the first to introduce the Norman castle. The accession of the Norman Duke William to the English throne in 1066 sparked the widespread introduction of the earth-and-timber ringwork and motte-and-bailey castles by the new Norman lords, built to consolidate the conquest. These hastily built works had a surprising permanence: for example, Windsor Castle began as a Norman motte-and-bailey castle. Others,

Canterbury city walls: a fourteenth-century handgun position replacing an earlier arrow slit.

such as the Tower of London, were built from new in stone, in this case within the existing Roman walls of the city of London. Other castles, such as Old Sarum in Wiltshire, made use of prehistoric earthworks. The later, great Norman stone keeps of the twelfth century are now thought to have been built more as an expression of Norman lordly status than as primary defence works. The alarming rise in the number of such private castles led later English kings to attempt to limit their growth by the issuing of Licences to Crenellate. The keep-and-bailey design would be gradually replaced in the thirteenth and fourteenth centuries by concentric castles, such as Caerphilly Castle or the unfinished castle of Edward I at Beaumaris on Anglesey. Greater emphasis began to be placed on water defence by the use of moats in order to give protection against the mining of castle walls and also to distance the castle from increasingly powerful siege engines.

Gunpowder was probably invented in China in the first millennium AD and the knowledge of its properties reached Europe in the middle of the thirteenth century. The first cannon appeared in Europe in the early fourteenth century. Charcoal, saltpetre and sulphur were the constituents of gunpowder; the first could be manufactured in Britain, but sulphur and much of the saltpetre had to be imported (Sind in what was then India provided most of Britain's saltpetre in the nineteenth century). The advent of this revolutionary recipe also gave an advantage in that the monarch could begin to control the bulk of its production, this process being completed in Britain by the eighteenth century. At this time, too, the production of artillery passed from private hands with the establishment of the Royal Brass Foundry at Woolwich.

In the mid fifteenth century the French, in the latter stages of the Hundred Years War, had employed as siege engines early forms of cannon known as bombards that could, with ease, demolish the high and relatively thin walls of the castles held by the British in France. In 1494 Charles VIII employed in his wars in northern Italy a well-organised siege train of cannon that could destroy any opposing castle. It quickly became apparent that the future of fortification lay in works that were lower, with stone or brick walls backed by impact-absorbing earthen banks and with wide and deep moats and ditches.

The appearance of artillery led to the adaptation of existing English fortifications to take cannon or handguns in the later Middle Ages. The walls and gates of Canterbury and the castle of Cooling, also in Kent, with their inverted keyhole-shaped gunports, and the Welsh castle of Raglan with its dual arrow slits and gunports are examples of existing or new fortifications adapted for cannon or handguns. However, there is not complete academic agreement as to whether these adaptations were merely for show or were expressions of a need to provide up-to-date security. The longbow and crossbow would, however, remain in service beyond the reign of Henry VIII. The new artillery works appeared in fortifications in those parts of England that faced the traditional enemy – France – or in the ports and harbours of the east, south and west that were subject to random attacks from foreign privateers. Gunpowder artillery also made an early

Devil's Point Blockhouse, Plymouth: an early-sixteenth-century artillery blockhouse.

5

Ravenscraig Castle, Fife: begun in 1460 and the first fortress in Scotland designed solely for artillery and handguns. Inverted-keyhole-shaped slits cover the bridge, with typically Scottish, widely splayed embrasures for artillery above. The round tower and high walls still evoke a medieval aspect, however.

appearance in Scotland, which was often the scene of dynastic feuding: one of the earliest castles designed from the start for both defensive and offensive artillery is Ravenscraig, near Kirkcaldy, begun in 1460. Another fifteenth-century Scottish artillery castle is that at Blackness. The late-fifteenth- and early-sixteenth-century small guntowers built to protect the harbours of Fowey and Dartmouth are other examples of early dedicated artillery fortifications. At the beginning of the sixteenth century new guntowers were also built in Scotland at the castles of Dunbar and at Tantallon, the latter also showing defensive earthworks dating from a siege of the seventeenth century.

For much of the period described, the works of fortification reflected the English and later British policy of opposing any continental power that sought to control the English Channel from ports in France, Holland, Belgium or north Germany, and from which an invasion of southern or eastern England might be launched. King

Blackness Castle, Falkirk: a strong artillery tower of the fifteenth century. Widely splayed gun positions in the base of the tower cover the interior of the castle.

Tantallon Castle, East Lothian: a modern replica of an early-sixteenth-century cannon on a simple wooden bedstock, positioned behind an original, circular gunport.

Philip II of Spain, Louis XIV, Napoleon Bonaparte, Kaiser Wilhelm II and Adolf Hitler were to suffer significant reverses or frustrations. The only periods in which Britain's fortifications were actually locked in a struggle were during the English Civil War and the Jacobite rebellions of the eighteenth century. From the beginning of the twentieth century control of the air above the country also began to assume importance with the onset of powered flight.

The period covered by this book is marked by the often hurried building of fortifications, in many cases massively expensive in terms of money, materials and labour, in times of threat. They were often obsolete before their completion, after which followed long periods of neglect and decay. For most of the period covered by this book the nation's primary defence would remain the moat of the English Channel and Britain's powerful navy.

Tantallon Castle, East Lothian: the dovecote and, beyond the outer ditch, the seventeenth-century triangular ravelin for mounting artillery, giving additional defence in depth. North Berwick Law is in the background.

2

Henry VIII's 'Great Castles' and Elizabethan bastions

The quarter century before the accession of Henry VII in 1485 had seen bloodshed and the violent departure from the throne of three kings. Henry Tudor would usher in a period of relative tranquillity. His teenage son, Henry VIII, came to the throne in 1509. A decade later Charles V of Spain, the nephew of Henry's first wife Catherine of Aragon, was elected Holy Roman Emperor. To pre-empt a French alliance with the Emperor, Henry allied his country with France, despite his earlier wars with that country. The divorce of Henry, once named by the Pope 'Defender of the Faith', from Catherine in 1533 led to a breach with Rome, exacerbated by Henry declaring himself head of the Church of England. The Pope encouraged the idea of an invasion of England and in 1539 the Emperor and Francis I of France signed a truce and Spain began to assemble an invasion fleet. England was now isolated and its shores were threatened with landings launched from continental ports.

Henry strengthened his navy and began an ambitious scheme for the construction of artillery fortifications, his 'Great Castles'. The plan was to complete a chain of forts, blockhouses and gun batteries to protect the harbours and potential landing-places of his nation. Since his youth Henry had been fascinated by the study of artillery and fortifications. He had been the author of a plan for the refortification of Calais in 1532 that was an attempt both to modernise existing fortifications and to develop new works by the reduction in height of wall towers and the creation of platforms for cannon. Similar schemes were not unusual in the 1530s: Norham

Pendennis Castle, Cornwall: the 1540s keep, gun battery and slightly later (1550) northern entrance block, which provided the governor with comparatively palatial accommodation.

St Mawes Castle, Cornwall, with a nineteenth-century gunpowder magazine in the right foreground.

Castle in Northumberland, after falling to a Scottish incursion in 1513, had been remodelled for artillery use. Henry's new forts, in their pleasing geometric forms and their concentration on all-round offensive and defensive firepower, were the equals of anything seen in continental Europe at that time, far removed from such late-medieval residential fortifications as Herstmonceux in Sussex. This would be the first major scheme of fortification since Edward I's castles in North Wales of the late thirteenth century. The work was begun in great haste, the appointments of local commissioners being made in March 1539. Of the principal works twenty-four had been completed and garrisoned by the end of 1540 and, with the exception of the Cornish works of Pendennis and St Mawes, all of the work had been completed by 1543. Large numbers of men were employed: at Sandgate in Kent 630 men were working in the summer season, the number dropping to one hundred in the winter season.

These handsome works were technically further advanced than anything seen before in England. They had a consistent design philosophy, were well built with massive and mainly rounded walls, and were equipped with widely splayed cannon embrasures and gun-smoke vents. Their design provided excellent all-round coverage of the surrounding area and the lobed bastions and parapets were designed to deflect missiles. The central keep mounted on its roof heavier-calibre guns for use against shipping. The outer bastions (Deal, for example, had six) were generally rounded in shape and open-backed, the latter a feature perhaps inspired by the open-backed towers of the Middle Ages. An enemy gaining the outer defences would find he had little cover from the fire directed from the inner layer or layers. On their roof platforms further guns could be mounted.

The first step in the construction of most of the works was often the building of the central keep, with the outer layer or layers following later. The different levels of gun position made the forts amenable to their different defensive and offensive roles, the lowest layers being for handguns or light artillery against enemy soldiers. The lower parapets were fitted with shutters for protection, vents for the evacuation

9

of smoke and slots for the handguns. The large castle at Deal had 145 embrasures, far more than its meagre allotment of guns, but the contemporary introduction of wheeled guns now meant that guns could more easily be moved about the works. In an emergency guns could be mustered from elsewhere to be mounted in Henry's 'Great Castles'.

England had in the past relied on guns made in the Low Countries, generally of bronze, but in the light of its isolated situation a burgeoning gun-founding industry was established in the 1540s based on London and the Weald of Kent, use being made of Wealden iron ores and charcoal. Guns were now cast and not forged and there had been improvements in the reliability of gunpowder. Pendennis Castle had a small number of modern culverins firing a 5 pound (2 kg) iron ball the distance of a mile (for the next four hundred years the calibre of a gun would often be expressed in terms of the weight of its projectile, one pound equalling 0.4536 kg). In 1547 the castle contained twenty-six guns, although these were mainly of the obsolete wrought-iron type. In addition to artillery and handguns Henry's works still made use of the longbow for close defence.

The major effort went into the works on the south coast of England, facing France, the ports of the West Country having earlier artillery fortifications to protect them from privateer attack. Deal, Walmer and Camber were built to protect the important anchorage of the Downs; the largest work, Deal, had a garrison of one captain and thirty-four troops and gunners. In the event of invasion these numbers could be increased by a local muster of men. The River Thames, a highway to the capital, was not neglected as small blockhouses were built along its course at East Tilbury, Tilbury, Gravesend, Higham and Milton. It is believed that these largely now-vanished works (the foundations of the Gravesend blockhouse remain visible) were designed by James Needham and Christopher Morice and adopted a D-shaped plan with the curved section mounting artillery and facing the river. Milton was remodelled by Sir Richard Lee in 1545 and provided with angled bastions; it was among the first in England to be built in this revolutionary form.

Fortunately for Henry and his nation, the threat from Europe was short-lived. The treaty between Charles V and Francis I soon broke down, and in 1541 France and the Empire were at war. Henry allied himself with Charles. In July 1545 Francis launched a short-lived attack on the Isle of Wight: Henry's 'Great Castles' were mustered for fear of further attacks, but these did not materialise as the continental rivals were becoming increasingly involved with their own national problems.

Henry's ability to start his ambitious scheme of works so quickly was influenced by a number of favourable factors. The dissolution and sale of monastic lands after the papal breach generated large amounts of money for the state, and he was also helped by his inheritance from his father of a healthy treasury surplus emanating from Henry VII's prudent fiscal policies. Another advantage was the availability of large quantities of cut stone and timber, lead and other materials from the monasteries confiscated by the state. Deal Castle, for example, was built of Caen stone probably looted from a local monastery.

In addition to protecting likely landing-places, the King's defences, in their varying designs, were also built to protect important harbours such as Falmouth, Weymouth, Rye, Hull and Milford Haven. A number of paired forts were built, for example those covering river mouths such as St Mawes Castle and Pendennis Castle, each protecting the entrance to the Carrick Roads. In addition to the works already mentioned, castles, blockhouses and artillery batteries were built along the south coast at Sandown on the Isle of Wight, Dover and Sandgate in Kent, Calshot and Hurst in Hampshire and at Portland in Dorset. On the Isle of Wight two 'cow towers' were built, their name living on in the local place-name of Cowes. The scheme was extended by the artillery fortifications at Harwich in Essex, Hull in East Yorkshire, Portsmouth in Hampshire, and Poole in Dorset. At Hull Henry modernised the medieval city walls: John Rogers, recalled from Calais, built in 1542 two blockhouses and the

Above: *Portland Castle, Dorset: the open, lower gun positions, and the curved parapet of the keep.*

Hurst Castle, Hampshire: the octagonal keep.

Hurst Castle, Hampshire: the lobed front of one of the gun positions in this Henrician work incorporated into the later fortifications.

castle. These works were similar in design if not size, consisting of a square keep and two rounded bastions. With the exception of the later castles at St Mawes and Pendennis, those built from 1540 moved from the lobed form of the earlier castles to a simpler, more rectangular plan. Southsea Castle in Hampshire, built in 1542, adopted an angular plan: improvements in the range of fortress cannon over those that could be carried in warships pointed to the fact that the rounded, shot-deflecting bastions were no longer necessary.

We do not know the names of all of the military engineers who designed and built these quite distinctive works. It is likely that Henry VIII would have taken an active interest in their design and progress. A Moravian engineer, Stephan von Haschenperg, has been identified with the design of the castles of Hurst, Calshot, Sandgate and Sandown and with the later phases of Camber Castle. He was also involved with the construction of the earthen artillery bulwarks between the Downs castles, together with artillery works at Carlisle Castle. The Half Moon Battery remains of this work to protect an important border castle. Beyond this we have little information on who designed and built England's first dedicated artillery fortifications.

Henry referred to his works as his 'Great Castles' and they retain the description of castle rather than artillery fort. They were built in response to an invasion threat and were not, unlike the medieval royal and baronial castles, in any sense lordly residences. Their role was to deny to an enemy's shipping, by virtue of their artillery, suitable landing-places or anchorages. They were also designed to defeat any troops who might gain a foothold: they were therefore largely built near the beach level. Accommodation, except for that of the captain or governor, was quite basic, the gunners sleeping and messing among their guns, as was the custom aboard warships at that time. The officer was provided with separate accommodation in the keep, with a fireplace, kitchen and private toilet. Water was provided in the form of a well or by a cistern fed by rainwater. Their utilitarian nature did not mean that they lacked any form of ornamentation; for example, elaborate stone and wood carving can be seen

Carlisle Castle, Cumbria: the sixteenth-century Half Moon Battery (foreground), a remaining part of the Henrician artillery defences of this strategically positioned castle.

at the castles of Pendennis and St Mawes, both having loyal inscriptions composed by John Leland, antiquary to the King.

The provision of moats, rounded bastions, pointed arches, drawbridges and portcullises in Henry's fortifications still evokes a faintly medieval feel. However, they quickly became outmoded: their profiles were too high and vulnerable to the increasing power of land-based artillery. They required too many guns, and their curved bastions created dead areas of ground. Soon they would be superseded by the revolutionary developments in fortification design coming from Renaissance Italy. However, they continued to play a part in the defence of Tudor England, especially during the Armada scares. Also, their situations were well chosen, and several, such as Hurst and Pendennis, would be incorporated into later schemes of fortification, their active lives even extending into the Second World War and beyond.

The revolutionary arrow-headed bastion, the work of military engineers such as the Italian Sangallo the younger, were first developed in Italy in about 1500. Their design would influence the setting out of the defences of towns, cities and other strong points for the next three hundred years. From their ramparts artillery could be mounted to fire into the field, and the faces of adjacent walls or flanks could also be swept by shot: there would be no dead ground. Artillery could now be moved more easily from place to place in the fortress, improving the efficiency of the work and reducing the number of artillery pieces required. Their drawback was that their strictly geometric shape made them unsuitable for rocky or undulating ground. The first indications in England of this new style appeared in the mid sixteenth century in the new works at Southsea, Portsmouth, Tynemouth and Sandown. A very early, solitary and vestigial arrowhead bastion can be seen on the landward side of the new fort at Yarmouth on the Isle of Wight built in Henry's reign in 1547, two years after the French attack on the island. The guns covering the two landward faces were recessed into the flanks of its only bastion. These early works were constructed of stone but a cheaper and more effective remedy against the advance of artillery power

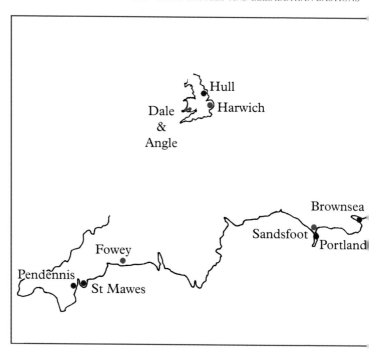

soon appeared in the form of relatively thin stone walls revetting bastions and walls of impact-absorbing earth. Breaches made by enemy artillery could be filled in an emergency with earth or whatever materials were to hand. The profiles of such works became lower, often hidden behind a gently sloping glacis, and in time extensive outworks and water defences would appear.

The accession of Elizabeth I ushered in a new era, but it was not, unlike her father's reign, remarkable for the construction of many new coastal defences. The Queen's policy of clever diplomacy unravelled when she assisted the Protestant Netherlands in its war with Spain. In 1558 Spain prepared for invasion, but the fortifications of Henry VIII had become neglected, or even, in the case of the Kentish blockhouses at Milton and Higham, demolished. One major work was built in Elizabeth's reign and this was the scheme to provide new walls for the border town of Berwick-upon-Tweed. Within the walls, with their five mighty bastions, were accommodation for a garrison of forty soldiers, a powder magazine, stores, a blacksmith's forge and stables. It was not Elizabeth who had instigated the work but Mary Tudor, who instructed the military engineer Sir Richard Lee in 1558 to design a modern system. The works built at Berwick were the equal of any on the Continent at that time. The work proceeded slowly, coming to a halt, incomplete, in 1569.

The need for such English border fortifications would diminish with the anticipated accession of James VI of Scotland to the throne as James I of England in 1603, resulting in the unification of the two thrones. The end of the century brought a run-down in both the navy and the national stock of fortifications. However, some further work in bastioned form took place late in the century at St Mawes and Pendennis (designed by Paul Ive, who had had experience in the Low Countries) and at Carisbrooke on the Isle of Wight. Here a much earlier fortification was modernised

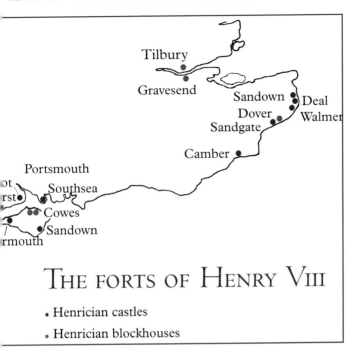

THE FORTS OF HENRY VIII

- Henrician castles
- Henrician blockhouses

Yarmouth Castle, Isle of Wight: one of the earliest English works to display a bastion, in this case the solitary one on the left of the castle.

Berwick-upon-Tweed, Northumberland: one of the great Elizabethan bastions with its two flanking gun positions.

Below: *Pendennis Castle, Cornwall: the seventeenth-century entrance into the Elizabethan bastioned fort, constructed on the orders of Sir Walter Raleigh and enclosing one of Henry VIII's 'Great Castles'.*

Upnor Castle, Kent: built by Queen Elizabeth I as part of the Medway defences, and whose batteries engaged a Dutch fleet in the seventeenth century. The view shows the landward side with the river on the extreme right: 'storm poles' (anti-scaling devices) have been recreated on the parapet. These were sharpened stakes set horizontally on a rampart to prevent or disrupt any attempt by infantry to storm a stronghold.

by the building of a bastioned trace designed by the Italian engineer Genebelli, who also designed star-shaped traces for the Henrician forts of Tilbury and Gravesend.

Another famous Elizabethan, Sir Francis Drake, built a bastioned fortress on Plymouth Hoe in 1595. Other fortifications were built at Upnor, Kent (also designed by Lee), Harry's Walls and Star Castle on the Isles of Scilly, and in the Channel Islands at Mont Orgueil Castle on Jersey and Castle Cornet on Guernsey. Lee's work at Upnor was something of a hybrid, quite different to his work at Berwick, with a single large angled bastion beside the Medway, slim and round stair-towers and a lofty barrack block.

Scotland in the sixteenth century had its own foreign policies and alliances and no national scheme of works was felt to be required. Private tower houses and castles continued to be built and be provided with

Star Castle, St Mary's, Isles of Scilly: a small, bastioned, star-shaped fort of 1593.

17

Craignethan Castle, South Lanarkshire: the ditch caponier of c.1530 with its three widely splayed embrasures.

St Andrews Castle, Fife: the modern entrance (foreground) to the mine and countermine galleries of the siege of 1546.

St Andrews Castle, Fife: the point at which the underground countermine and siege mine gallery met.

small inverted-keyhole or wide-mouthed gunports for handguns or small artillery pieces. However, evidence of the influence of continental developments can be seen in the batteries at Dunbar and Stirling Castles and in the defences of Eyemouth, Dunglass and Craignethan Castle. At the last a substantial wall, provided with four wide-mouthed gunports, faced the ditch, within which was an early form of caponier. Here, handguns fired from canted gunports down both lengths of the ditch: a lack of ventilation would have meant that the caponier would have quickly filled with powder smoke. Nor was the medieval castle dead in Scotland: the powerful castle of Tantallon comfortably withstood an artillery siege in 1528.

3
The English Civil War

Apart from the works of Henry VIII and the limited projects of Mary and Elizabeth, the art of fortification in Britain at the beginning of the seventeenth century had developed slowly after peace had been agreed with Spain in 1604 by James I. However, it was a different situation on the Continent, where the Thirty Years War (1618–48), and especially the long struggle between the Dutch and their Spanish occupiers in that war, had encouraged the extensive employment of military engineers. Some, for example the Stuart kings' principal military engineer Sir Bernard de Gomme, born in Flanders, would also bring their talents to British service.

In the early part of the seventeenth century major improvements in military organisation had taken place during the wars in the Netherlands, particularly under Prince Maurits of Nassau, principally in the construction of military camps, the more regular payment of soldiers, and especially in drill. These reforms were incorporated into the continental military manuals of the time. The period also brought improvements in the design of ordnance and new patterns of fortification, such as the use by the Dutch of extensive water defences and outworks. During the devastating continental wars also came the introduction of large standing armies, a feature that would make its appearance in England and Wales during the civil wars. The Dutch and English experienced a love-hate relationship in the seventeenth century: there was intense commercial rivalry despite the religious sympathy for the Protestant Dutch in their wars with Catholic Spain. Many English and Scottish volunteers or mercenaries had fought on the Dutch side against Spain: it has been said that between 1626 and 1632 almost one tenth of the Scottish male population had been involved in this fighting. On their return to the British Isles the volunteers would exercise a major influence in the formation and running of Cromwell's New Model Army, formed in the spring of 1645, and many future commanders on both sides received their military training in the continental conflicts. At the same time the military engineer took on a greater significance and European countries began to acquire their own experts, for example Vauban in France and Stevin and Coehoorn in the Dutch Netherlands. In England Sir Bernard de Gomme was, like his counterparts working on the Continent, effectively an architect, a field surveyor and a mathematician, determining designs together with the layout and angles of bastions and the lengths of curtain walls.

The developing feud between Charles I, who held the view that he had a divine right to rule, and his Parliament over religious and other matters came to a head in August 1642 when Charles raised his standard at Nottingham, the traditional gesture of a monarch about to wage war. The more modern fortifications at the start of what would become known as the 'English Civil War' were generally those located about the coast, although the remainder of the country retained many medieval castles and walled towns and cities. Although referred to as the 'English Civil War', the bloody conflict was in three stages and also involved Wales, Ireland and Scotland. The whole of the nation became a potential battleground. Towns and cities became isolated in enemy territory: Parliamentarian centres such as Boston, Hull and Plymouth held out during sieges despite being in regions of Royalist support. On the other hand, Colchester (which was the subject of a particularly brutal siege during the second civil war), King's Lynn and Newark were isolated and besieged in Parliamentarian country, the last holding out for four years.

The Civil War developed into a protracted struggle to hold and conquer territory, especially in the form of cities and towns, fertile lowlands, the main roads and ports.

Military, administrative and financial control was exerted through a string of local strong points, these containing the principal garrisons and armouries, which also acted as centres for local defence and attack. These strong points were often the medieval castles and walled towns and cities around the coast, or those overlooking river estuaries, or straddling main routes or borderlands. Strongly built manor houses and even cathedral closes came to be put into a defensible condition during the conflict. After a long period of relative peace, many of Britain's castles had been abandoned, and castles were generally considered unfashionable and uncomfortable, if not downright unnecessary. Some had lingered on in use as prisons or as administrative centres; for example Ludlow Castle in Shropshire housed the Council in the Marches of Wales. Others were retained as the seats of powerful families after sometimes extensive remodelling, such as at the castles of Kenilworth in Warwickshire, and Powis and Chirk in Powys. Many of the remainder had become roofless shells, but their walls and gatehouses were often still strong and could be quickly repaired by re-roofing to accommodate guns and garrisons. Additional strength was added to many sites by banking earth behind or in front of their walls, or by the construction of a bastioned trace of earth to mount guns and so girdle the whole site.

The rapid development in cavalry tactics and artillery technology and its use led to a more mobile form of warfare. The 24 pounder culverin could demolish stone fortifications and over 15 feet (4.6 metres) of earth was required to absorb its iron shot. The culverin and its smaller relation the demi-culverin had ranges of over a mile and a half and as a consequence new defences were increasingly required to be pushed forward of the main work. The smaller artillery pieces on these forward works, such as the saker, could fire a 5 pound (2 kg) shot for over a mile. Heavier guns, such as the cannon royal, had, because of their weight, to be located on firm ground or on stout wooden platforms. At Huntingdon the Norman castle mound provided both a stable and an elevated site: the ramp up which artillery was pushed can still be seen. It was also during the civil wars that the bomb-throwing mortar first made a limited appearance. With a short inclined barrel fixed at an angle of not less than 45 degrees, and with a range dictated by the amount of its gunpowder charge, the mortar could drop an exploding bomb into the interior of a fortification with devastating effect. This had been demonstrated during the siege of the city of Chester.

The preliminary actions in the first part of the Civil War involved two of the most up-to-date works of fortification in the country – those at Hull and at Portsmouth – and early actions also involved attempts to seize arsenals. Hull had declared for Parliament, as had the navy, and so Hull and other Parliamentarian ports could continue to be supplied by sea and also be protected by the navy. Portsmouth, on the other hand, declared for the King, was blockaded by the navy and bombarded from two positions, one of which was the captured Southsea Castle, a Henrician artillery castle. The garrison quickly surrendered. Elsewhere, the medieval walls of such towns as Northampton were reinforced by earthen ramparts in the late summer of 1642, and the arsenal of Manchester resisted, despite its only defences being hastily erected earth walls and chain-blocked streets, the King's forces withdrawing ignominiously.

As the war developed, so did the art of siege warfare. The experiences of Henry Hexham and Robert Ward, among others, in the continental wars were published respectively in *The Principles of the Art Militare, as Practised in the Warres of the United Netherlands* and in *Anima'adversions of Warre*. These were to influence both the manner of fortification and the means of its reduction by siege during the coming conflicts. The first stage in any continental siege would be the isolation of the fortress by the building of two rings of fortification: one to encircle the fortress (circumvallation), the other to protect the besieger's rear (contravallation). Then trenches would be dug towards the fortress and gun batteries would be established close to its walls. The next stage would be the construction of zigzag trenches called saps (to avoid enfilade fire) towards the ditches of the enemy's fortification. The final stage before the storming of the work was the construction of causeways across the ditches to support timber galleries. These would be moved up to any breaches in the walls caused by the besieger's cannon, or be used as a shelter for the attachment of an explosive mine to the base of the wall. Such a mine was used to demolish part of St Mary's Tower on York's city wall during the Parliamentarian siege of 1644; the subsequent repairs may still be seen. Mining played a part during, for example, the sieges of the city of Gloucester and at Old Wardour Castle in 1643, and at the castles of Sherborne and Pontefract in 1645. At Pontefract three countermine shafts dating from the siege can still be seen: these were driven from the castle in an attempt to intercept the besiegers' mining operations towards the castle walls. Oliver Cromwell's New Model Army contained a large siege train, and this favoured the technique of heavy bombardment and assault rather than more indirect methods. Sieges undertaken by the New Model Army were, consequently, of shorter duration but were considerably bloodier. Of the 645 military actions in the civil wars it has been estimated that 198 involved sieges, with artillery coming to play an increasing role. Parliament also had the advantage in controlling the Weald of Kent, the principal iron-producing, and therefore gun-founding, area.

In October 1642 the King turned towards London, its medieval walls having been urgently repaired and an 18 mile (29 km) long scheme of outer defences erected by volunteers against the monarch's approach. The defences consisted of ramparts and ditches connecting twenty-one small forts and redoubts of earth (often referred to as 'sconces' in the civil wars), which blocked routes into the city and protected the main fresh water supply at Islington, as well as the Thames docks. The small earthwork fortifications of the conflict took their inspiration from those shown in the continental military manuals: the preferred design was the palisaded and ditched sconce. This was often provided with a gateway and a drawbridge and was usually of a square or pentagonal plan with bastions for the mounting of cannon at each corner. Pitfalls and other traps designed to disrupt an infantry or cavalry charge could be dug on the approaches to the sconce. The King's forces failed to make any progress in the face of the London defences and withdrew towards Reading and ultimately the Royalist stronghold and power base of Oxford.

The East Midlands and East Anglia were the locations of Oliver Cromwell's earliest campaigns: he would become the leading military and political figure on the Parliamentarian side. In March 1643 he completed the refortification of Cambridge

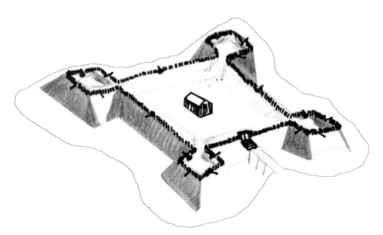

Simplified sketch of a Civil War sconce. The walls are of palisade (wood) and cannon sit on the four bastions. A wooden magazine occupies the centre of the sconce.

The Queen's Sconce, Newark, Nottinghamshire: a view taken from the top of one of the four earthen bastions of this Civil War fort, with its deep ditch to the right. The interior of the sconce is to the left.

Castle: cannon on new bastions were positioned around the castle, which was reported at the time as being very strongly fortified with 'breastworks and bulwarks'. By 1646 it was run down and left with a small garrison of two sergeants and twenty-five soldiers. (It is interesting to note that in 1940 the city's anti-invasion defence plan also involved the refortification of the castle with road blocks, barbed wire, trenches and pillboxes.) Bridges around the town were demolished, with a line of defences pushed beyond the original medieval city walls. The main Royalist threat to Parliament in the East Midlands, however, was at Newark, this town being in a strategic position astride the Great North Road and at a crossing point of the River Trent. Newark, after two unsuccessful sieges by Parliament, was progressively strengthened with a ring of defences outside the town's medieval walls, including ditches, hornworks, bastions, redoubts, pitfalls, palisades and stockades and powerful artillery sconces, for example the King's Sconce and the still-extant Queen's Sconce. It is possible that the military engineer Sir Bernard de Gomme, who had accompanied Prince Rupert from the Continent to aid Charles I, played a part in the design of the defences, especially the Queen's Sconce. The extent of Newark's defences and siege works was as impressive as any constructed on the Continent at that time.

In August 1643 Oliver Cromwell became governor of the Isle of Ely and it is likely that Horsey Hill Fort and Earith Bulwark, both of which remain, were built by him to control the Fen Causeway, with other forts also controlling the southern approaches to East Anglia. Earith Bulwark controlled the bridge over the Old Bedford River and the Great Ouse. It was square, ditched and with a bastion at each corner for artillery. Cromwell gave up Ely in 1644, retreating to Peterborough. Cromwell's home town of Huntingdon was fortified, a span of the river bridge demolished and a drawbridge inserted. We have previously seen that the town's castle was reused for cannon, and the town's churches were also used as observation posts or converted into strong points, a use often repeated elsewhere in the country. The town nevertheless fell to Charles in August 1644.

In January 1644 the Scottish Covenanters had joined the King after he brought his army back from Ireland, having made peace with the Irish rebels. In April 1644 the

Earith Bulwark, Cambridgeshire: thistles mark the line of the ditch of the Civil War sconce, and in the right foreground sits a Second World War Allan Williams turret on one of the bastions. Made of steel, the rotating turret was designed to take two men and a light machine-gun; it formed a ready-made armoured defence post. The fort provided a handy, elevated site for the 1940 anti-invasion defences covering the Ouse crossing.

siege using the greatest numbers of men took place outside the walls of the Royalist headquarters at York. The walls were still in relatively good repair, and sconces covered the approaches to the main city gates, upon which were mounted cannon. After three months of resistance the King's garrison surrendered in July 1644, shortly after Charles's disastrous defeat at the battle of Marston Moor in Yorkshire.

The hasty fortifications at, for example, London lacked the facility of flanking defence and later works would apply more scientific (and continental) principles, approaching in design the carefully thought-out bastioned defences of Elizabethan works, for example those at Berwick-upon-Tweed. The King's defences around Oxford (designed by Sir Bernard de Gomme) and at Newark included mutually supporting forts (sconces) and bastion-shaped entrenchment positions. At Oxford the surrounding towns such as Banbury and Woodstock were also fortified to give defence in depth. Before the siege of Oxford had begun in earnest in June 1646 the King had fled the city, this event and the loss of Newark in April 1646 effectively ending the first civil war. However, some Royalist garrisons held out for the King well after the end of the main conflict, for example those at Pendennis Castle in Cornwall, and at the Yorkshire castles of Skipton, Scarborough and Bolton.

The hastily constructed earthen and timber bastioned defences generally fared well against the relatively light artillery of the time. The earth absorbed the impact of cannon-balls, and the bastions, projecting into the field, supported artillery protected behind gabions of earth and stones or stout wooden palisades. For example, Basing House in Hampshire, built within the banks of a Norman ringwork castle, was hastily surrounded by earthen bastions and was besieged for over two years, its site dominating the road from London to the West Country. In October 1645, tiring from its interference of his communications, Cromwell launched a devastating assault and breached its defences.

At Gloucester archaeological excavation has demonstrated the development of an important city's defences during the struggle. In 1642 Parliament had repaired the medieval walls, reinforcing their backs by building earth banks against them, while some of the city gate towers had been filled with earth on which to mount guns. Additional ditched and bastioned defences were dug around the city by its citizens,

Chester city walls: Civil War remodelling of the medieval city wall parapet is apparent here, carried out to create emergency gun embrasures.

incorporating in part the local topography, for example by using a local watercourse as a barrier. Two sconces were built to cover the main approaches to the city, while excavation revealed the presence of the Royalist saps and mines. Where dwellings might give an enemy cover, these were destroyed; over 240 houses were demolished in the suburbs of the city in August 1643. In that month the defences came under artillery fire and Royalist sappers started to build a mine under the east gate, protected by a musketeer-filled timber gallery. The mine was to no avail as heavy rain filled the galleries and the Parliamentarian garrison launched doughty counter-attacks. The approach of a relieving army signalled the end of the siege of Gloucester.

Donnington Castle, Berkshire, with Civil War artillery earthworks and evidence of post-siege repairs to the medieval gatehouse.

In the summer of 1643 the King again attempted to take London, this time by a three-pronged attack, hoping to eliminate the major Parliamentarian garrisons in his way. However, a stout defence, for example that undertaken earlier in the war at Manchester, could often compensate for weak fortifications. Bristol fell after a siege (one fifth of the population dying during it) and in August the King moved against and invested the Parliamentary garrison at Gloucester, defended, as previously mentioned, by its medieval walls and weak earthworks. One breach in the walls was efficiently and effectively filled with woolsacks. When the garrison was at its last gasp the King withdrew on 5th September 1643. The King's other forces approaching London from the north were also held up by Parliamentarian attacks out of Hull, while in the west Prince Rupert's forces were held up for over a month by the stout resistance offered by the defenders of the weakly fortified Lyme Regis. Charles had failed to take the capital once more.

Let us look now at an area of Britain in a little more detail, discussing the role of its fortifications in the civil wars. Wales was, arguably, the predominant place in which the medieval castle saw extensive reuse; over thirty Welsh castles were involved in combat during the war, many maintaining lengthy sieges. Traces of contemporary defences may still be seen in Wales, for example in the arrow-headed earthen bastions built at the castles of Raglan, Carew and Manorbier. Remains of one of the unique fortifications of the war – the sconce – can be found near Caerphilly Castle, appropriately on the site of a Roman fort. In Wales the majority of the gentry declared for the King, the principal exception being the castle and medieval walled town at Pembroke, which remained throughout the conflict the main Parliamentarian power base in the principality. At the beginning of the seventeenth century England had relied on a long-established amateur defence system of county militias and trained bands, but the system was in decay. In Wales at the start of the war the King had given instructions to the gentry to raise their own infantry regiments. Commissioners of Array were appointed to recruit, equip, feed and, it was hoped, pay the new soldiers. To produce the necessary coinage for this payment, the King, having lost his principal mint in London, established new mints such as that at Aberystwyth. To provide the silver, much of the gentry's plate was melted down.

Despite advances in artillery, the castle in the mid seventeenth century often remained a formidable obstacle and any attempt at a daylight frontal attack by infantry was likely to be almost suicidal. Therefore, other means of taking a fortress had to be found; for example, Powis Castle fell to a night attack by Parliament in October 1644, while a bribe secured the capture of Chirk Castle in 1645. Where other means had not proved a success, siege methods were resorted to. In 1644 and 1646 trenches were dug and batteries positioned to isolate and bring about the surrender of the castles of Montgomery and Raglan. Surrender might be engendered, too, by starvation, or by the fear of starvation, this occurring during the reduction of a number of Edward I's castles in 1646 and 1647. Explosive mines were positioned under walls, such as those used against the castles of Monmouth and Ruthin. If the besieger was able to get sufficiently close a petard might be fixed to the gate, as at Powis Castle, but the most common form of attack involved the use of intense artillery bombardments, often directed against a weak spot. This caused Chepstow Castle to fall in 1645, and, after its recapture, again in 1648. Many fell after long, arduous and bloody sieges, for example at the castles of Holt and Harlech, where there were nine-month-long investments. If well supplied with powder and provisions, a garrison of as few men as twelve could hold a castle for a considerable period of time. The heavy artillery required to carry out a successful siege was relatively scarce and also somewhat unreliable, as well as being cumbersome and difficult to move along the country's primitive road system. Even prolonged bombardments sometimes had little effect, for example those directed at Pembroke Castle and town.

A less obvious form of building called into use in Britain during the conflict was the church. Small artillery pieces could be mounted on the tops of church towers, these also acting as observation posts, and church naves were convenient for the storage of gunpowder, horses and other stores. The Welsh border church of Stokesay in Shropshire is such an example, used as a war store and damaged by Parliamentary forces during the brief siege of the nearby castle in the summer of 1645.

In September 1644 the capture of Montgomery Castle opened up mid Wales to the advance of Parliament's forces. The castle, on its strong hilltop position, was of considerable importance as it was the gateway to the upper Severn and mid Wales. It was the property of Lord Herbert of Chirbury, whose stance in the war had been largely neutral. Parliament called upon Herbert to surrender after having fixed a petard to the castle gate: he promptly carried out this demand and the castle surrendered, to be occupied by five hundred Parliamentary troops. The Royalists built siege works in preparation for the besieging of the castle, manned by over four thousand men, while Parliament sent a similar force to relieve the castle's garrison. In the battle below the castle the Royalists were defeated, the loss of men and gunpowder consequently leading to the severe depletion of the Royalist garrisons at Liverpool, Chester and Shrewsbury. The next objective was Powis Castle: a petard blew in the outer gate, leading to the equally rapid surrender of the Royalist garrison. Denbigh Castle was considered to be too strong to attack and the Parliamentary force moved on to Chirk, working away at the base of the castle's walls with picks and crowbars under the protection of a wooden shelter, but heavy stones dropped from the ramparts drove them off.

By the spring of 1644 a significant number of the South Wales castles had been taken from Parliament, but this was to be short-lived. Parliament retook the castles of Pembrokeshire effortlessly, but not that at Laugharne, Carmarthenshire, which was described as 'one of the holds from where our forces and the country received the greatest annoyance'. The castle had been modernised and made more comfortable in the seventeenth century but it still remained defensible. It fell in the autumn after a siege of one week, the Parliamentarian troops and artillery having been brought from London by sea to the port of Milford Haven. The castle refused to surrender when called upon to do so. The first attempts put the artillery too far from the castle, but after the capture of the town's outer defences, including the town gate, guns were moved on to the gate, where they bombarded, breached and captured the castle's outer bailey. The Royalist garrison retreated to the inner bailey, but a threat to mine the walls led to its surrender.

The Royalist cause started to collapse in Wales in 1645 and 1646. In July and August 1645 Charles was in Wales, residing principally at Raglan Castle. Parliament had captured the Royalist strongholds of Chepstow and Monmouth by October 1645, with only Raglan remaining in royal control. The castle was an early-fifteenth-century work provided with both arrow and gun loops but had been additionally fortified in the civil wars with angled bastioned defences on its vulnerable south-eastern front. It had a strong garrison, was well supplied and possessed a deep moat and thick walls together with its new outer works. In the summer of 1646 a siege began, lasting for thirteen weeks. The besiegers dug trenches and installed a gun battery on high ground overlooking the castle. This proceeded to bombard and gradually destroy the Royalist cannon mounted on the towers of the castle. A little later, mortars throwing 12 inch (305 mm) bombs, including one brought from Hereford called 'Roaring Meg', were brought by Parliament to the siege. Surrender was finally induced by the threat to use the formidable mortars, and by the digging of saps that began to approach closely upon the castle's walls. Raglan surrendered in August 1646, the besiegers finding only one barrel of gunpowder remaining, although the garrison had managed to make a powder mill within the castle during the siege.

By the beginning of 1646 South Wales, apart from stubborn Royalist garrisons such as those at Raglan, was in Parliament's hands. The northern English Marches had been lost in the previous year. Parliament then moved north: in June 1646, in the same month that Charles had ordered those places still resisting to surrender,

Raglan Castle, Monmouthshire: the Great Gatehouse, showing evidence on its parapets of the destruction wrought in the Civil War. Note also the original, small late-medieval circular gun embrasures covering the entrance.

the Edwardian castle of Denbigh was subjected to bombardment, this being directed at the Goblin Tower, which was believed to be the site of the castle well. The castle held firm but on Charles's order the garrison surrendered in October. Caernarfon and Conwy followed suit, the latter surrendering after a three-month-long siege. Harlech Castle, because of the rocky nature of its site, was able to remain defiant with only a garrison of twenty-eight men. The first civil war in Wales was effectively over with the surrender of Harlech in March 1647.

After leaving Oxford in April 1646 Charles had fled to Scotland but was handed into Parliament's custody in 1647. The King was detained but fled to the Isle of Wight, reaching an agreement with the Scots that they would send an army south to his aid. The second civil war began in 1648, but the Scottish army achieved little, being defeated at Preston in Lancashire. In the meantime there had been considerable discontent with Parliamentarian rule in South Wales, and rebellion began there in 1648 and its castles and walled towns were once more involved in conflict. Pembroke, declaring for the King this time, was besieged for seven weeks in the summer of that year. On its surrender, the Royalist leader of the town was executed. This was one of a number of outrages committed by both sides on prisoners during the wars: for example, a number of Charles's Irish troops were hanged after the surrender of Shrewsbury Castle, and there was a particularly brutal massacre at Hopton Castle in Shropshire. But at Portland Castle in Dorset the garrison had been allowed to leave with colours flying. The Welsh rebels were defeated at the Battle of St Fagans in May 1648 and two months later Chepstow Castle's walls were breached by Parliament, the guns for the siege having been brought from Gloucester and Bristol. Charles was executed in January 1649 and in May 1649 the Commonwealth was established, Britain becoming, briefly, a republic.

In July 1650 the executed king's son, Charles Stuart, landed in Scotland. That year his Scottish army had been defeated at Dunbar by the New Model Army, and, following this, the fortresses of Stirling, Edinburgh, Dirleton, Borthwick and Tantallon were taken by General Monck for the Commonwealth. To secure Scotland further against more internal upheaval, Monck also built five modern bastioned forts: Ayr Citadel, Oliver's Fort at Inverness, Inverlochy, Leith and Perth, plus a number of smaller forts. In January 1651 Charles was proclaimed by the Scots as Charles II, and in September 1651 he moved south, beginning the third civil war. He stopped at Worcester; within days the city was surrounded, the Royalist army was defeated and Charles fled to the Continent.

Most of Britain's permanent fortifications not subjected to damaging sieges survived the first war relatively intact, although many of the temporary earthwork and timber defences appear to have been quickly demolished and their ditches filled in. Despite this, there still remain many, if only insubstantial, traces of the earthworks erected by both sides in the wars. Partial demolition (slighting) was often carried out by both sides, especially after the abandonment of the fortifications, in order to deny them to the other side. From 1648 onwards Parliament adopted a policy of authorised slighting, a list of the garrisons to be maintained or works to be slighted having been put to the Commons for agreement. Some slighting, for example that at Helmsley Castle in Yorkshire, was agreed but not carried out until after the end of the second civil war (the Royalists had, in the meantime, re-garrisoned the castle at the start of the second war). On slighting, a section of Helmsley's keep was undermined and a huge section of wall brought down, the curtain walls also being reduced in height, effectively ending this castle's role as a place of strength.

The destruction of the fortifications

After the conclusion of the second civil war, Parliament had ordered more demolitions. Some were carried out in an overzealous manner: at Aberystwyth the castle was almost completely destroyed by the use of prodigious quantities of gunpowder, while at Pembroke Castle gunpowder charges were placed in the basements of towers in order to blow out their fronts. The castles at Chepstow and Ludlow, on the other hand, were repaired and used as prisons. At Montgomery Castle 150 labourers, together with numbers of miners and carpenters, were employed in its lengthy destruction, all usable materials being carefully removed for reuse. At other castles alternative means were used; for example, Raglan's Great Tower was undermined, propped, and the props were then fired, bringing down a section of its walling. The moat was also drained to further slight the site. Scarborough Castle required a company of foot for the work, which, in the event, was never completed, the castle remaining a place of strength into the nineteenth century. The restoration of the monarchy in 1660 did not stop the damage: Beaumaris, Conwy and Denbigh, for example, were stripped of their valuable lead and timber during the reign of Charles II. Money could also flow in the wrong direction. At Goodrich Castle in Herefordshire, which had received the attentions of 'Roaring Meg' in 1646 and where some subsequent slighting of the castle had taken place, the Countess of Kent successfully lodged a claim for compensation for the damage and was awarded £1000. There could be a punitive element in the choice of sites, too. For his support of the Royalist cause Sir Thomas Myddleton lost one-third of Chirk Castle, demolished by the Commonwealth, his family being forced to live elsewhere until the castle was repaired for habitation. Other owners were paid to demolish their own strongholds, and county committees were formed to consider the extent of the demolition works, while others, in order to keep their properties, made indemnities that these would not be used against the Commonwealth in any future conflict. In the event, there was an underestimation of the sheer physical task of the planned slightings, and there was also a mounting fear of many potentially expensive legal suits. After the initial enthusiasm to destroy what many thought of as the embodiment of the nation's suffering, the orders began to be ignored.

The principal areas in which slighting was conducted on a large scale were Wales, Yorkshire and the Midlands. We have seen that the destruction did not stop at the Restoration, nor was it confined to castles alone: cities that had supported Parliament, for example Gloucester, had parts of their city walls demolished. On the other hand, Britain's more modern coastal fortifications were kept relatively intact as it was felt by the Commonwealth to be wise to retain these for the nation's security. The fighting days of the medieval fortifications in England and Wales were now largely over and most would, in the future, remain mere romantic ruins. In Scotland and Ireland there was no comparable level of demolition and the traditional tower house would remain in use for habitation into the eighteenth century and beyond.

4

The Restoration and the work of de Gomme

In the civil wars a significant proportion of the actions involved sieges of castles, walled towns and other strong points. The relatively few modern, pre-existing bastioned fortifications, situated around the coasts of the kingdom, had seen little fighting. Some additional works of coastal fortification had been carried out to resist Dutch raids during the war with Holland in 1652, for example Cromwell's Tower in the Isles of Scilly. Further conflicts with the Dutch occurred in the periods 1665–7 and 1672–4, and there was risk of war with France in 1678. The Dutch were developing a modern fleet, intending to challenge British naval supremacy. However, by the late seventeenth century, under Charles II's encouragement, an expanding British navy was emerging to meet the Dutch challenge, Charles having inherited the efficient Commonwealth navy. The new navy, now called Royal, required its bases and docks to be protected and a limited scheme of refortification was begun in Charles's reign. Chatham, close to the capital, was the main naval base, with the fleet anchorage being at the Nore off Sheerness, while Plymouth and Portsmouth were the two other principal dockyards. The Ordnance Office (later the Board of Ordnance) was responsible for both works of fortification and barracks, and since the later Middle Ages it had supplied guns and ammunition to both the army and the navy. After the Restoration of Charles II in 1660 it had become involved in the programme of refortification with the King's active interest.

After the flight of Charles I from Oxford in 1646 his military engineer, Bernard

de Gomme, was given permission by Parliament to leave the country, returning at the Restoration in 1660, when he was appointed as the engineer in charge of the King's fortifications. In 1665, at the time of the second Dutch war and at the height of the Great Plague, de Gomme was granted leave to travel and to attend to the urgent improvements at Harwich, principally at Landguard Fort, this and the town having successfully resisted the Dutch Admiral de Ruyter. From Harwich he travelled to review the fortifications of Portsmouth and Plymouth.

Despite peace talks, in June 1667 the Dutch decided to attack again. Their fleet was sighted off

Tilbury Fort, Essex: the fine, monumental gateway of de Gomme's fort, flanked by baroque martial designs.

Tilbury Fort, Essex: a replica gun of the sixteenth century on the ravelin fronting the Landport Gate. A pair of lifting bridges controlled access across the moat to the fort.

the Thames but the Medway defences failed to stop them, the Dutch breaking the Chatham boom chain and being free to roam at will among the fleet, damaging both ships and shore defences. The only effective defences were the batteries about Upnor Castle, guns having been hastily rushed there from the Tower of London. After peace was agreed, the fort at Sheerness was reconstructed and the refortification of the Medway began. In 1670 de Gomme was at Tilbury, in the later 1670s he was busy strengthening the defences of Portsmouth, and in 1681 he was at Hull. In 1682 he was appointed Surveyor General of Fortifications. His chief surviving works are the Royal Citadel at Plymouth, completed in 1680, and Tilbury Fort, described in more detail below, at both of which opulent gateways display the influence of the baroque period. Plymouth Citadel, like Tilbury, was provided from the outset with permanent barracks (the first British barracks had been established under the Commonwealth by General Monck at the new citadels built to control Scotland) and it still retains a garrison of Royal Marines. This bastioned work dominated not only Plymouth Hoe and the town but also one of the principal channels, the Cattewater. De Gomme's work may also be seen at Her Majesty's Tower of London (Legge's Mount), although some of his other works are now in a fragmentary condition: Sheerness's bastioned trace is now almost lost, Cockham Wood Fort has slipped into the Medway, and the nearby Gillingham Fort is now also lost. Small traces of his work remain at Portsmouth and Gosport too.

In 1670 de Gomme was commissioned, in the light of the Dutch debacle, to build a powerful fort on the Thames at Tilbury, east of London. Built on continental lines, it was reminiscent, in its low-lying watery site, of the Dutch fortifications so familiar to de Gomme. Its plan was pentagonal, displaying four landward bastions, with water-filled moats crossed by drawbridges via a redan and a ravelin, and between the moats a covered way for infantry. While its main purpose was to house a battery to block the Thames, the landward defences had been given thorough attention. Piling was required to support the walls and bastions in the marshy ground conditions and Norwegian wood was imported for this purpose: some of the piling for the fifth, uncompleted, riverside bastion remains visible at low tide. Instead of this bastion, a powerful gun battery was built along the riverside. The fort was so designed that

Aerial plan of Tilbury Fort, Essex, with the River Thames in the background.

A. Places d'armes
B. East gun line
C. East bastion
D. Officers' barracks
E. Landport gate
F. Water gate
G. West bastion
H. West gunline
I. Inner moat

J. Outer moat
K. North-east bastion
L. Covered way
M. Magazines
N. Ravelin
O. Redan
P. Outer bridge
Q. North-west bastion

the moats could be quickly drained, as otherwise, in freezing weather, it might be possible for an enemy to move across the ice covering the moat and so reach the fort's walls. The bricks left over from its building were used in the construction of the Greenwich Observatory. In its later history it was used as a transit camp for army regiments, but it was never considered to be a salubrious posting: the damp and marshy conditions engendered fevers and there was no supply of fresh water within the fort. The year 1776 was one of the few occasions when the fort was the scene of aggressive action, when a county cricket match was held on the parade ground. The match ended in disagreement and injury, one of the soldier players being bayoneted and another shot!

A surviving seventeenth-century sentry box at Hull Citadel, now re-erected.

After de Gomme's visit in 1680, Hull Citadel was started the following year, not to his own design but to one by the Swedish engineer Martin Beckman. On visiting the port Beckman had found the Henrician fortifications 'in total ruin'. He repaired the castle and one of the blockhouses and built a new triangular, three-bastioned citadel with a tenaille front by the River Humber, incorporating the earlier works. In 1745 a twelve-gun battery was built by the river, but all of the fortifications were levelled in the following century. The later defences of Hull were moved outwards towards the Humber estuary. As part of the 1860 Royal Commission report's recommendations Fort Paull Battery was built in 1864. Later defences included the two steel and concrete sea forts at Haile Sand and Bull Sand, built at the time of the First World War, plus coastal artillery batteries at Kilnsea and Spurn Point.

5
The Jacobite revolts

In sixteenth-century Scotland some limited bastioned work had been carried out, such as the English and French bastions (there had been a long and amicable relationship between Scotland and France, the 'Auld Alliance') at Eyemouth, but the kingdom was not sufficiently wealthy to afford major permanent fortifications in the new bastioned form. The first substantial bastioned work was General Monck's pentagonal fort at Inverlochy, one of the five such works built by him to control Scotland against Royalist insurrection. In the reign of Charles II Fort Charlotte was built in 1665 by John Mylne, his master mason in Scotland, to guard Bressay Sound, on the eastern side of the Shetland Islands, against the Dutch, the fort being burnt by the Dutch in 1673 and then rebuilt in the late eighteenth century.

Berwick-upon-Tweed, Northumberland: the eighteenth-century gunpowder magazine behind the town walls. The building has been given buttresses and a strong surrounding wall, designed with the intention of channelling any explosion upwards and away from the walls.

Berwick-upon-Tweed, Northumberland: elegant eighteenth-century barracks behind the town wall.

Edinburgh Castle: the impressive Half Moon Battery of 1574 sits in front of the castle proper.

In the 'Glorious Revolution' of 1688 the last Stuart king, James II, was deposed and replaced by the Dutch Protestant William of Orange and his wife, Mary. James fled to France and then to Ireland. The native Irish Catholic population was sympathetic to the Stuarts and a rebellion began. The momentum of the revolt was stopped by the resistance of the walled and bastioned city of Londonderry, established by the City of London Corporation in the early seventeenth century. The siege lasted 105 days, but it was at the cost of many thousands of dead on both sides. James's Catholic forces were finally defeated, after the unsuccessful siege of Protestant Londonderry, at the Battle of the Boyne.

The change of monarch had also been greeted with dismay by the Scottish Highland clans and their chiefs, who on religious, cultural and other grounds were also sympathetic to the Stuarts, and the first of a series of rebellions began in 1689. In March John Graham of Claverhouse, 'Bonny Dundee', was appointed by the deposed James II as his commander-in-chief in Scotland. Graham raised James's standard

against William III but soon lost Edinburgh Castle when its garrison surrendered. In July both armies met at the pass of Killiecrankie. Although the Government army lost most of its men, Graham was mortally wounded and without his leadership the rebellion subsided. In that same year the Grand Battery had been constructed at Stirling Castle, the key to northern Scotland, and in 1708–14 the castle also received a bastioned front as additional protection against the possibility of further Jacobite rebellions ('Jacobus' being the Latin for James). General Monck's old Cromwellian fort at Inverlochy, slighted with the other Cromwellian forts after the Restoration, was rebuilt by General Mackay in 1692 and named Fort William in honour of the King, and Inverness Castle was restored.

The city walls of Londonderry, showing one of the original cannon shipped to Londonderry in the early seventeenth century and bearing the City of London crest.

35

Ruthven Barracks, Highland: the imposing ruins of the Georgian barracks, provided with small musketry flanking positions, as well as firing positions in the walls of the barracks. The large building on the left was the stables for a party of dragoons, acting as an escort during the movement of money or provisions in the Highlands.

The next revolt was in 1715. The rebels hoped to take Edinburgh but Stirling Castle and its new battery successfully blocked their progress south. In 1717, as a consequence of the two previous revolts, four new lightly defensible barracks were built in the Highlands, the largest being at the southern end of Loch Ness where Fort Augustus was later to be built. Ruthven was the smallest of the barracks but remains in the best state of preservation. Seven years later General Wade began his famous road-building programme to enable the Georgian army to be moved more quickly about the Highlands: the lack of roads and bridges had materially helped the rebels. Wade's principal route ran down the Great Glen, linking the new forts of Fort George, Fort Augustus and Fort William. These new forts, designed by John Romer, were not, however, designed to resist a serious assault.

In 1719 came a further uprising, this time with Spanish assistance. The rebels'

headquarters were in the castle on the loch islet of Eilean Donan, this being quickly destroyed by Royal Navy warships that had gained access to the loch. It was made clear by this series of rebellions that the previous attempts at policing the Highlands had been inadequate, especially when foreign aid was made available to the Jacobites.

In spite of the rebellions there was much complacency in London. The last and most serious rebellion, which began in 1745, found the Highland forts undermanned or even unmanned, and they offered little resistance to the rebels, who referred to them contemptuously as 'toy forts'. The rebels moved south into England, capturing Carlisle Castle with little difficulty. Undefeated in battle, the

Ruthven Barracks, Highland: a detail of one of the flanking positions (officers' accommodation), firing along the wall of the barracks.

Fort George, Highland: view across the ditch with the decorative gateway to the far left, together with one of the flanking bastions with its stone sentry box to the right.

Jacobite army penetrated as far as Derby before a decision was made to retreat to Scotland. On the move north the Jacobites occupied Carlisle Castle briefly. The rebels maintained their retreat into Scotland but failed to take Stirling Castle in January 1746, thwarted again by the guns of the 1689 battery. More success awaited them at the fortified barracks of Ruthven, captured and then slighted with the aid of the barracks' own cannon. Reaching the Great Glen, and with Prince Charles Edward's headquarters at Inverness, the rebels set about reducing the Government's Highland forts. A mine was dug towards Fort George at Inverness, leading to the surrender of the fortress. At Fort Augustus a Jacobite shell fortuitously ignited the magazine's contents, after which the fort surrendered and it, too, was slighted. Only Fort William remained in the King's hands, its guns supported by the fire from the Royal Navy ships moored alongside the fort. The last rebellion was finally crushed at the Battle of Culloden in April 1746.

The relatively poor showing of the Hanoverian forts in the Highlands led to the construction of a new generation of fortifications. The Duke of Cumberland, a son of George II, requested replacements for the old Forts George and Augustus. The latter was on a weak site and had been merely rebuilt on similar lines to the earlier fort. The original site of Fort George had been too limited in area, so a new site was chosen on a peninsula at Ardersier, a few miles north-east of Inverness, the new site jutting out into the Moray Firth. The designer of the Fort George at Ardersier was William Skinner, the masonry and brickwork being contracted to William Adam, the

Fort George, Highland: model of the fort, showing the entrance and ravelin in the foreground and the space taken up by barracks in the fort's interior.

architect father of the more famous Robert and James Adam.

The new fortress remains one of the most complete and impressive of its type and period in Europe. It took twenty-one years to complete but the original plan was largely adhered to, indicating a competent initial design and designer. The site afforded an enemy little dead ground, and it could dominate the Moray Firth with its gun batteries. Although Fort George was overlooked by higher ground a mile (1.6 km) away, this was not a big problem at the time because the fort was beyond the effective capability of contemporary guns and howitzers. Although cannon fire could reach the fort, the power of the shot was vastly reduced at this extreme range. Four powerful bastions and two demi-bastions protected the curtain. The fort was approached across a glacis, then across a ditched ravelin, a bridge and drawbridge leading to the principal decorated and crested gateway. The ravelin's cannon and muskets protected the east curtain and a covered way ran around the glacis. Recessed assembly areas for infantry counter-attacks, known as *places d'armes*, were situated on the frontal glacis and by the lateral ramparts. Dominating the front of the fort were the two principal bastions, named after the Prince of Wales and the Duke of Cumberland. These and the other bastions contained brick embrasures for cannon as well as elegant stone sentry boxes on the corners of the bastions.

Building Fort George presented a number of challenges to Skinner. There were few local tradesmen, and so specialists had to be drawn from the Lowlands and elsewhere, and building materials were largely moved by sea. It was the greatest single work of construction in the Highlands at that time. One thousand labourers and soldiers, working in a hostile environment, provided the muscle power, and the wheelbarrows so necessary for the moving of earth were ordered in batches of fifty. By 1753 the ravelin was ready after acting as a temporary redoubt. As the work progressed the workforce was gradually reduced and by 1769 the fort was generally complete. Its principal armament in 1760 consisted of twelve 42 pounders, four 32

Fort George, Highland: the north casemated curtain and sallyport, leading to a place d'armes. Some of the fort's barracks can be seen on the left behind the curtain.

Fort George, Highland: a reconstruction of the barrack room providing accommodation for Private John Anderson and his wife. From the end of the seventeenth century a soldier had to obtain his commanding officer's approval to marry, and he and his wife would have to share a room with other, unmarried men. The sheet across the bed provided their only privacy.

pounders, twenty-one 18 pounders, twenty-two 12 pounders, four 6 pounders and two 13 inch (330 mm) mortars. By the 1770s the fort was considered by many as unnecessary, especially as, after the Battle of Culloden, the Highlands had become relatively peaceful.

Fort George was designed to hold two infantry battalions in artillery-proof ('bombproof') casemated barracks within the brick and earth ramparts. In times of

Carrickfergus, County Antrim, on Belfast Lough, showing early-nineteenth-century gun embrasures in this medieval castle.

peace the impressive barrack blocks filling the interior of the fort would be used. The fort became the principal base for the new Highland regiments, this role continuing to the present day. In the late eighteenth century it was garrisoned by a Regiment of Invalids, who must have been considered fit enough for the gentler duties of fort garrison life. To supplement and improve access to the new forts, by 1767 over a thousand miles of additional roads had been built in the Highlands and some smaller existing tower houses, for example that at Corgarff, Aberdeenshire, were converted into fortified barracks to hold additional garrisons.

Forts William and Augustus were sold after the end of the Crimean War, the former to become a railway depot, the latter becoming, ironically, a place of peace as an abbey. The small, detached fortified Highland barracks, however, remained in use for some considerable time and against a new enemy – those Highlanders trying to elude the excise men by smuggling or by the possession of illicit whisky stills. From the beginning of the nineteenth century bastioned fortifications such as Fort George were rapidly becoming obsolete: their largely defensive armament and vertical walls made them extremely vulnerable to the explosive shell in the middle of that century.

Despite the new works of fortification in Britain in the eighteenth and nineteenth centuries, some more ancient works remained in use. In the eighteenth century the Norman Carlisle Castle, for example, had formed part of England's defences against the possibility of invasion from Scotland. In 1745 it was occupied briefly by the Jacobites, who quickly surrendered the castle after a Government battery opened fire on their temporary quarters. The castle retained its earlier and inadequate artillery defences such as the sixteenth-century Half Moon Battery, which had been built to protect the inner gate. As with other castles, for example Portchester in Hampshire, it was used as a prison for Jacobite and French Napoleonic prisoners of war. The French Revolution had led the British Government to fear a growth in seditious activity by an often disaffected populace and in the 1790s the castle's guns were refurbished – although these would, in the event, be fired only for royal salutes!

In the early nineteenth century Carlisle Castle began to take on a new lease of life as a military stores depot; other Norman castles would be similarly used, Chester, for example, serving as a regimental headquarters into the twentieth century. War with Napoleonic France resumed in 1803 and there was considerable fear of invasion via Ireland or Scotland, both centres of political unrest. Carlisle Castle was still seen as serving a useful purpose in blocking any rebel movement southwards. In 1804 a new armoury was built, together with new infantry positions on the walls to protect this from the mob. In 1827 the arms and ammunition were transferred for greater safety from the magazine to the castle's inner ward, the armoury being converted into a barracks. The castle was also now accommodating, in a rough and ready fashion, two companies of infantry. In the late 1830s the Chartist riots broke out, and further internal barracks were built between 1836 and 1837 to house troops on internal security duties, as well as a new hospital. The risk of insurrection in the mid nineteenth century, incidentally, led to the provision of light defensive positions for many new or existing external barracks. As an aid to keeping the garrison fit a fives court was built at the castle, one of twenty-nine built by the army throughout the country, but the overcrowded conditions continued through the Victorian period.

Other earlier fortifications continued to function in an age of artillery: for example Carrickfergus Castle in Ulster maintained a continuing coast-defence role even into the Second World War, and the batteries about the great fortress of Henry III at Dover protected the Dover Straits well into the middle of the twentieth century.

6
War with France and Pitt's 'Pork Pies'

The Channel Islands, close to France, were a vital element in the movement and protection of British mercantile trade in the eighteenth century. Overall French power had been reduced after the conclusion of the Seven Years War and the expulsion of the French from North America and India. Nevertheless, in 1778 the French had bombarded Elizabeth Castle, and in 1781 a party landed on Jersey but it was repulsed; more protection for the islands was clearly required. Two important works were built: Fort George on Guernsey, finished in 1812, and Fort Regent on Jersey, finished in 1814. Earlier artillery fortifications on Guernsey include those built at Castle Cornet (with a bastioned front) and at Vale Castle, both of which were provided with artillery batteries. On Jersey Mont Orgueil Castle has a seventeenth-century battery and bastions. Elizabeth Castle has a bastioned trace begun in 1594 to a design by Paul Ive.

The accession of William of Orange had had continental repercussions too. Britain now allied herself with the Dutch cause and against Louis XIV, leading to two further wars, the War of the Grand Alliance in 1689–97 and the War of the Spanish Succession in 1702–13. Further conflict arose in 1740–4 during the War of the Austrian Succession, leading to an attempted invasion (with Maldon in Essex as the landing point), but the French fleet was defeated by a Channel storm. There was a further plan for invasion in 1756 during the course of the Seven Years War, with yet another plan and its ultimate defeat when the French invasion escort fleet was destroyed by the Royal Navy at Quiberon Bay in November 1759. The War of American Independence began in 1775. France was naturally sympathetic to an American rebellion against British rule and it was feared that France might take advantage of the fact that much of the British Army was fighting in America and mount yet another invasion. In 1778 the American adventurer John Paul Jones, with French assistance, attacked a number of British ports and succeeded in destroying a gun battery at Whitehaven in Cumbria. A Franco-Spanish plan was drawn up in 1779 for a fleet to clear the Channel in readiness for infantry landings along the Sussex coast, and also to attack and put Plymouth out of action. Planning for the invasion included assessments by French spies of Britain's fortifications: those of the city of Portsmouth, for example, were considered to be in good shape but undermanned. Again, an enemy invasion fleet was launched but this time it was defeated by an outbreak of sickness and disease, the fleet limping back to Brest in September 1779. Each invasion attempt so far had foundered on the weakness of the French navy.

After these emergencies had passed, a survey of the nation's defences was undertaken and much decay was found. Thirty new batteries were now planned, running from Great Yarmouth in Norfolk to Fowey in Cornwall, together with the refurbishment of existing batteries. New Tavern Fort in Kent, one of the new batteries, was built with sixteen guns concealed behind an earthen rampart, and there was a new battery built to face it across the River Thames at Tilbury. The lower reaches of the Thames were considered to be still highly vulnerable to attack. Earthen redoubts and batteries were also built at Plymouth: at Maker, Mount Wise, Western King and Cawsand. The Devonport and Portsea lines were constructed and at Dover new batteries were built and work started on an entrenched camp at the Western Heights to protect the landward approaches to the castle and to act as a marshalling

Dover, Western Heights: the Citadel underground barracks. Although flanked by musketry openings, the large windows of the barracks would have made them vulnerable to enemy cannon fire.

point for anti-invasion troops. Further work was carried on here between 1794 and 1805, strengthening the eastern defences. Four major detached works were built, connected by tunnels to Dover Castle, and an early form of nineteenth-century caponier protected the ditches. The work of strengthening Dover, at the shortest crossing point of the English Channel, carried on into the early nineteenth century. The Citadel was started, as well as the North Centre Bastion and the Drop Redoubt – all to be fitted with bombproof barracks. The remarkable Grand Shaft, designed by Lieutenant Colonel Twiss and comprising a triple spiral staircase, was built to facilitate the rapid movement of troops from the Heights to the harbour area. A 420

Fort Amherst, Kent: Napoleonic era gun drill.

feet (128 metres) deep well, almost as remarkable a work of engineering as the Shaft, provided the expanding garrison with fresh water.

The several invasion scares in the first half of the eighteenth century led to the need to protect the important and expanding dockyard at Chatham. Starting as the Chatham Lines, a mighty ditched defence was built running around the royal dockyard that would eventually develop into a complicated strong point of bastions, batteries and redoubts. The work on the Lines began in 1755, undertaken by the engineer J. P. Desmaretz, who was also involved in the upgrading of the Dover Castle defences, and was completed by 1820. However, the works caused some discontent at the time among the local population, who were no longer able to graze their stock or play cricket on the land now occupied by the Lines. These remain the only substantially surviving Napoleonic-era fortifications in Britain, outliving in use nearby contemporaries such as Forts Pitt and Clarence. They were even mentioned in Dickens's *The Pickwick Papers*, where the author describes the Royal Engineers' mock siege operations in the Medway area.

Amherst Redoubt and Townshend Redoubt were the principal strong points in the developed system of batteries, redoubts, caponiers, casemated barracks, outworks and flanking galleries, the whole eventually becoming known as Fort Amherst. Under Cornwallis Battery, on the eastern section of Fort Amherst, a vast network of tunnels and magazines was dug to provide barracks and stores in the event of a siege. The tunnels are among the fort's most striking features, running for nearly half a mile (800 metres) from the Cave Yard to underneath Cornwallis Battery. They were cut through the chalk, lined only intermittently with brick arches, and in the late twentieth century provided the location for some of the sequences in the film *The Mission*. Lateral tunnels connected with the gun galleries, originally armed with carronades, for covering the ditches with fire. Belvidere Battery contained the main entrance to the whole of the fort complex. It was entered via a loopholed guardroom, and through a courtyard provided with musket positions covering the ditch. Other batteries were located at Amherst Spur, at Prince William's Bastion and in the earliest part of the work at Amherst Redoubt, part of the original Lines. A large army of convicts completed the works: they also laboured in the brickworks that supplied the fortifications with the thousands of bricks necessary for their completion.

At the time of the Napoleonic Wars the ditch sides and the earthen ramparts were revetted in brick, and new magazines were built, the Lines eventually being extended to enclose part of the town of Rochester. Never completed, however, was a scheme to link up Forts Clarence, of 1812, and Pitt, of 1819, to Fort Amherst with a continuous line of ditches and ramparts that would have acted as a substantial barrier to any invader attempting to cross the Medway. The old fort's use was not over even in the twentieth century: in the First World War it acted as a depot for stores and troops en route to France. In the Second World War anti-aircraft defences were mounted on its ramparts, and it also formed part of the anti-invasion General Headquarters Line as the fort's deep ditches and high ramparts served as substantial anti-tank obstacles. Spigot mortars were positioned about the fort in 1941, as was a 4 inch (10 cm) gun in the salient of Prince William's Bastion, together with a 6 pounder anti-tank gun above the sallyport. The tunnels under Cornwallis Battery were taken over during the war as the headquarters of the Kent County Council Civil Defence Corps, air-conditioning being installed against gas attack, and this use continued into the 1950s. The fort also provided a training ground for the Home Guard in the Second World War and during the Korean War emergency.

Coastal defence, as a distinct branch of fortification engineering, had received limited attention after the reign of Henry VIII and before the nineteenth century, and yet it was of vital importance to Britain, with her naval and mercantile ports, dockyards, anchorages and harbours proximate to the Continent. During the Napoleonic Wars of 1803–15 the defence of the island was seen to rest mainly with the navy and in the raising of large armies rather than in the building of fortifications.

Coastal defence, therefore, was often seen as a poor relation and it was the navy that received the bulk of the Board of Ordnance's funds. After each conflict fortress guns were allowed to decay, but after every major war with France the country again turned to its coast artillery batteries for protection. Temporary loss of command of the Channel had occurred in the years 1667, 1690 and 1779. In the last of these years a Franco-Spanish fleet had anchored at Cawsand Bay near Plymouth and temporary batteries had been built after the emergency, as well as some permanent works. In an emergency temporary batteries could be hurriedly built and guns removed from warships to supplement the permanent land or floating sea batteries. The location of the batteries often depended on the geography of the entrances to harbours; for example, at Plymouth there was the advantage of a winding channel with 90 degree turns to slow an enemy's ships, and with the potential of placing batteries on the angles.

While in the eighteenth century Britain's fortifications were still stagnating, the many overseas wars had led to new developments on the Continent. At the end of the century the French Marquis de Montalembert advocated ideas that would lead to the eventual demise of the bastioned trace. He pointed to the need for the concentration and separation of offensive and defensive fire, and he was also in favour of caponiers and the use of casemates to protect artillery pieces and their crews. He further recommended the use of guntowers for close coastal defence: we shall see how Britain developed this idea in the nineteenth century. Montalembert saw that the flat curtain walls of the bastioned trace were becoming increasingly vulnerable to concentrated artillery fire; the design of the trace also helped to disperse artillery about the work rather than concentrating it where it might be needed most. This new way of thinking would eventually be adopted in Britain, although the bastioned trace was not yet dead.

In 1794 the new Fort Cumberland, covering Langstone Harbour at Portsmouth, and the last bastioned fortress to be built in England, introduced casemated guns designed to sweep its dry ditch, as well as sallyports for active defence. It faced across the harbour to its neighbour, the also new, casemated but vestigially bastioned Fort Monckton at Gosport. The two caponiers in the ditch at Fort Monckton reintroduced a defensive measure that would remain a feature of British fortifications for another hundred years. Andrew Saunders in *Fortress Britain* points to the importance of Forts Monckton and Cumberland in the gradual modification of the earlier bastioned system and the movement towards Montalembert's ideas in the identification of separate defensive and offensive systems.

The French Revolutionary War began in 1793, marking the start of twenty years of war between Britain and France. France, with her powerful army, looked again at mounting an invasion. Anticipating the threat, work began on new fortifications, especially in eastern Kent. Eleven artillery forts of a simple triangular shape, together with numerous gun batteries, were built between Deal in Kent and Eastbourne in Sussex. In 1796 Spain also declared war on Britain; a simultaneous war with two powerful countries was a situation that Britain had always tried to avoid. In the year that Spain declared war there was an unsuccessful attempt at a landing at Bantry Bay in Ireland, with another attempt in 1798. In 1797 a French force was able to land at Fishguard in Wales: their intention before capture had been to sack Bristol and then march north and sack the ports of Liverpool and Chester. The rapid mobilisation of local forces quickly put an end to this, the last actual invasion of the British mainland. The small and weak fort at Fishguard, however, played only an inauspicious role in the defeat of the enemy. The continuing threat to British security was such that in April 1798, for example, a pamphlet was circulated entitled 'Hints to assist in the general defences, London etc'. This stated that in the event of an invasion barricades would be provided for each street in the capital; the corner houses would be provided with hand-grenades; members of the livery companies would be armed; and there was seen to be a need to expel 'all noxious foreigners'.

Weedon, Northamptonshire: the walls, bastion and warehouses of the Board of Ordnance depot, accessible from the Grand Union Canal, and also serving as a royal refuge.

A demand for yet more coastal batteries arose throughout the kingdom, with, for example, three new batteries being built between 1796 and 1799 to protect the upper reaches of the Thames at Coalhouse Point in Essex and at Shornemead and Lower Hope Point in Kent. With four 24 pounder smooth-bore guns on traversing platforms, mounted on a semicircular rampart, they were provided with internal barracks, magazines and defensible gorges. Walnut trees were planted close to the batteries, providing not only food but also wood that could be used for the replacement of musket stocks. As an extra refinement the officers' quarters were furnished with wallpaper!

The next invasion threat would be of an entirely different order, however. Hardly a year had passed following the conclusion of the Revolutionary War with France before, in 1803, Britain declared war on Napoleonic France following that country's invasion of the Netherlands. Conscious now of an ever-greater risk of invasion, Parliament took the step of voting funds for a royal and defensible refuge at Weedon in Northamptonshire, this also serving as a large inland ordnance depot. France made preparations again for an invasion: the beaches from Folkestone to Dymchurch in Kent and from Rye to Hastings and Pevensey Bay in Sussex were considered by the Government to be the most likely landing areas. The south coast was again turned into an armed camp, with troops deployed to meet the landings. A French invasion force was drawn up in the ports between Holland and Le Havre, where a fleet of over two thousand small boats was prepared to be launched at Britain: a blockade of these ports took place. Eighty thousand French troops gathered at Boulogne for the crossing. In October 1805 a combined French and Spanish battle fleet emerged from the continental ports to attempt to force a passage for the invasion vessels, but the fleet was defeated at the Battle of Trafalgar. The prospect of an imminent invasion was now over and the French troops that had been earmarked for the operation were diverted to fight in Russia in aid of their Austrian allies.

The several French invasion scares, emerging more critically at the start of the Napoleonic Wars in 1803, prompted a review by the Government of the defences of

45

Folkestone, Kent: one of a line of Martello Towers. Another, light-painted tower can be seen in the background.

the south and east coasts. In that year a scheme was put forward by Captain Ford of the Royal Engineers to Brigadier General Twiss, Commanding Engineer Southern District, for a chain of mutually supporting towers, mounting cannon, along the Kent and Sussex coasts as a protection against French coastal landings at places between Folkestone in Kent and Eastbourne in Sussex. Ford's view was that the towers, eventually to be known as Martello Towers, would form stand-alone defence posts without the need for any adjacent gun batteries, and this view prevailed when the towers along the south coast were built. However, the Commanding Engineer's view was that the towers should form defensible keeps for adjacent batteries; there seemed, in his opinion, little advantage in their being isolated and without gun batteries. This view was adopted when the east-coast towers were built, these being provided with adjacent batteries.

'Martello Tower', then, is the familiar name for the round towers built by Britain between 1796 and 1860, although the towers built in the south and east of England tend to be regarded as the 'true' Martello Towers. The design of the towers originated during actions in the French Revolutionary War in Corsica in 1794, when a sixteenth-century Genoese stone tower held by the French at Mortella Point had put up a strong resistance. HMS *Fortitude* and HMS *Juno* had bombarded the tower for two hours to little effect, although the few cannon on the tower caused significant injury to the British ships. Only after troops had landed with field artillery was the tower subdued. The tower gave its name, in a slightly altered form, to the Martello Towers, which, in their general shape at least, followed the Corsican pattern. Among the earliest towers built were those erected between 1798 and 1802 by the British on the island of Minorca and considered at the time to be a success both militarily and economically. The next group of towers was built in the Channel Islands and Ireland, followed by those designed by Captain Ford for the south coast of England.

The work of building the towers was supervised by the Board of Ordnance, which, as we have seen, was also responsible for the building of all barracks and forts, as well as the provision of arms for the army and navy. The chairman of the Board was often a powerful and influential figure, the Duke of Wellington being one notable example. The Inspector General of Fortifications, in effect the army's senior engineer, commanded the Royal Engineers and the Royal Artillery, together with the Royal Sappers and Miners. He was also responsible for general fortification planning and the drawing up of budgets, while the Engineer officers prepared individual designs and supervised the work in the field.

The original plan was for eighty-eight towers. Building began in 1805, although by then the threat of invasion had diminished somewhat. In the event, by 1810 seventy-four towers had been completed, stretching to Seaford in Sussex, but

Martello Tower (number 61), near Pevensey, East Sussex: Second World War positions are apparent on the roof of the tower.

none was built towards Eastbourne. The towers were numbered from one, which was at The Warren, Folkestone, to seventy-four, at Seaford. Sandgate, one of the 'Great Castles' of Henry VIII, was brought up to date and converted into a form of Martello Tower by the insertion of a bombproof roof, although it was not given a number.

The continuation of the Napoleonic threat led to an extension of the Martello system along the east coast up to the edge of the East Anglian sea marshes, twenty-nine being built between Clacton in Essex and Aldeburgh in Suffolk, with work beginning in 1809. The eastern towers were lettered from A to Z, plus AA, BB and CC. The last of these towers, at Aldeburgh, was the most northerly and was built to a more elaborate design. It had vaulted internal arching to support the four roof guns and no central pier. It was designed to be surrounded by the sea and to be able to cover with fire all points of the surrounding ground. The land gap between the tower at Aldeburgh (CC) and the next tower (BB), 10 miles (16 km) to the south, was not considered to be vulnerable to a landing as it contained the marshy estuaries of the rivers Alde and Ore.

Aldeburgh Martello Tower, Suffolk: an unusual variation on the Martello Tower theme, being larger and of a quatrefoil plan for four roof-mounted guns. Most of the ditch wall that surrounded the tower has now been lost.

Right and below: *The locations of surviving Martello Towers are indicated by red letters or numerals. Based on W. H. Clements, 'Towers of Strength'.*

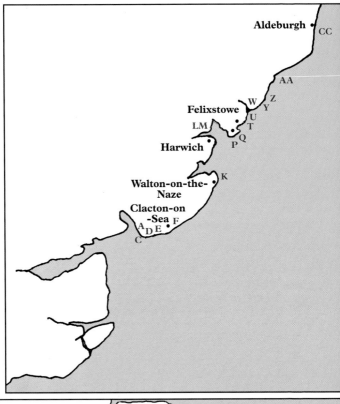

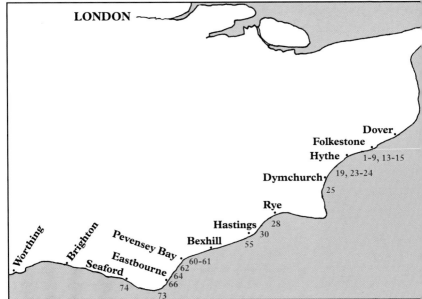

Eastbourne Redoubt, East Sussex: the circular wall of the redoubt and a caponier covering the base of the ditch.

As an additional defensive measure circular redoubts, absorbing large quantities of manpower, materials and weapons, and of doubtful value, were built at Eastbourne, Dymchurch and Harwich, armed with 24 pounder smooth-bore guns on their roofs, their ditches being protected by small caponiers. The Harwich Redoubt differed somewhat from the other redoubts in origin and purpose. At Harwich the presence of a small hill to the south of the town had always made it vulnerable to any enemy artillery that might be mounted on the hill. To deny this advantage to a potential enemy, and also to cross fire with Landguard Fort, Harwich Redoubt was built. The

Eastbourne Redoubt, East Sussex: the interior showing the parade ground, gun platform and casemated barrack accommodation.

49

Harwich Redoubt, Essex: the interior, showing the entrance (centre left) and adjacent roof gun positions.

work was planned by Major Bryce RA and apparently inspired by the French Fort Tigné on Malta. The original design was for an eight-gun, nine-sided redoubt. This was soon changed to a ten-gun circular redoubt, and in 1806 a Mr Frost of Norwich was appointed as principal contractor. A similar tower had been planned at Aldeburgh but, to save money, Martello Tower CC was built instead. Although its granite foundations had been laid by 1807, work on Harwich Redoubt proceeded at a slow pace. Progress was affected by the need to divert the London to Harwich road, there was also a general election at the time, and the production of the large numbers of bricks required for its building was slow. Work stopped for the winter, restarting again in 1808. By 1810 the redoubt was finished, although the cost had risen two-and-a-half times above the original estimate. It was designed to accommodate six officers and 250 men and its life was uneventful, although it was partly remodelled as a result of the 1860 Royal Commission, its gun embrasures being rebuilt in granite to give better protection for the gun crews. The final armament in the late nineteenth century consisted of three 9 inch (229 mm) rifled muzzle-loading guns. In the early twentieth century these guns were unceremoniously dumped in the moat and replaced by two 12 pounder quick-firing guns.

In Kent the shingle Dungeness peninsula, together with Romney Marsh, presented a barrier to an enemy's movement of artillery from his landing craft. However, the area was still felt to be vulnerable to infantry infiltration. To give the beach protection, the redoubt at Dymchurch and four batteries were built. In addition a defensive canal, acting as a barrier to an enemy's movement by cutting off the base of the peninsula, was proposed, running from Shorncliffe in Kent to Hastings in Sussex. When completed in 1809 by the leading canal builder John Rennie, it was named the Royal Military Canal. It runs for over 26 miles (42 km) and was provided with a military road, facilitating the movement of troops, artillery and supplies. The crossing of the canal was by means of movable wooden bridges. Gun batteries were positioned at each of the salients in the staggered sections of the canal to form, in effect, a defended moat. Martello Tower number 30, situated somewhat inland, protected the sluices that controlled the canal's water levels while six other towers guarded the sea sluices. In the Second World War the canal gained a new lease of life when it was incorporated into the area's anti-invasion defences as a water-filled anti-tank ditch and provided with pillboxes at its salient points.

Each south-coast tower was designed, usually, for one roof-mounted 24 pounder smooth-bore muzzle-loading cannon on a 360 degree, fully traversing platform. On some towers short-range cannon called carronades were provided where the surrounding ground was broken and could not be covered by the main armament. The 24 pounders had 20 degrees of inclination, the front wheels of the gun platform resting on a racer (a circular metal track) running at the base of the tower's parapet. The rear wheels of the carriage ran on a narrower racer, encircling a metal pivot, often formed of a metal pin set in an obsolete cannon barrel. On firing, the gun ran up an incline on the carriage so as to reduce the overall recoil. Movement of the weapons was by the use of ropes attached to the guns and fixed to metal hoops on the inside of the parapets. The east-coast towers, with the exception of Aldeburgh, which had four bays, had trefoil-shaped roofs with a pivot in each bay for their trio of cannon.

At the start of the Martello Tower programme in 1804 fourteen million bricks were ordered from the London builders' merchants Adam & Robertson, who subcontracted the supply to eleven brickworks in the south-east of England. Between 250,000 and 300,000 bricks were required to build each tower. It is not surprising to learn that some contractors made fortunes from the contracts. The final total cost of all of the towers was £350,000, an enormous sum at the time. The typical construction features of the true Martello Tower (also sometimes referred to as 'Pitt's Pork Pies', Pitt being the Prime Minister of the time, 'pork pie' because of their shape) are an elliptical (south-coast) or cam-shaped (east-coast) plan with a tapering profile. All of the English towers had walls that were thicker on the side facing the sea – that is, on the potential enemy's side. The towers at Seaford and Aldeburgh were isolated and were not part of the chain of self-supporting towers: consequently they were provided with their own ditches for greater protection. The towers built in England were of brick with the use of cut stone for doors and windows, and the walls were rendered in stucco. The brickwork was bedded in a mortar of lime, ash and hot tallow designed to give a very strong and waterproof bond that, in most cases, has resisted severe ageing. Entry into the towers was via a door at first-floor level, situated on the rear face, and reached by a ladder or, in the case of those with a ditch, by a drawbridge. The interiors were often damp. Access into the basement, where the magazine (often recessed to keep the powder dry) and provisions were kept, was via a ladder from the first floor. The tower's water supply was also here – a water tank filled from an external source, or a cistern fed by rainwater collected on the roof. The first floor had planks radiating from the central roof-supporting pillar, the floor containing the garrison's living quarters including a fireplace and a window. A staircase led to the roof, and ammunition was passed via the staircase to the roof gun or guns. However, the number of contractors, subcontractors and Royal Engineer officers involved in the construction of the towers often led to minor design and dimensional differences.

Garrisoned by up to twenty-four men and an officer, the towers, provisioned with food, water and ammunition, were capable of withstanding a siege for several days. None of the English towers saw action in its original role, although in the Second World War some were used as battery observation posts for emergency batteries or, in their original roles, as armed beach-defence positions. Many have been converted into homes, museums and tourist information centres.

Further examples of the Martello Tower were built in Scotland, Ireland, Canada, Sicily and the Adriatic before the Napoleonic War ended in 1815. In Ireland a network of towers was built around the coastline to warn of and to prevent the approach of parties of dissident Irishmen, reinforced by French or American volunteers, the first towers being built around Dublin Bay in 1804 shortly before the first English examples were built. With the exception of a solitary square example, all were circular

Magilligan Point Martello Tower, County Londonderry: an Irish tower of stone with a machicolated musket gallery above the entrance.

but to a design somewhat different from that of the English Martello, being of a smaller diameter and with a machicolated gallery above the entrance. Because of the lack of a central pier, their armament was often lighter, consisting of a single 24 or 18 pounder gun. One of the last Irish towers to be built, between 1812 and 1815, is that at Magilligan Point, Northern Ireland. Larger than its English contemporaries, of stone, with a machicolated musketry position over the entrance and armed with two 24 pounders, it was provided with a shot furnace. This was designed to heat metal cannon-balls red-hot, the intention being to ignite the sails, rigging or other combustible materials on an enemy ship. This tower also had the luxury of an internal spring of fresh water. The majority of the Irish towers survive; that at Sandycove near Dublin is the most famous, being the setting for the opening chapter of James Joyce's *Ulysses*.

In Scotland the Board of Ordnance proposed in 1807 a tower at Leith, the port for Edinburgh, but this was not to be completed for a further thirty years, possibly because the onus for its building was put on the city's corporation. The plan was for a large stone tower supporting three 32 pounder guns, with one officer and twenty-one troops as its complement, but the guns were never fitted. It was originally built on a sea-girt islet but is now encircled by a new pier. Elsewhere in Scotland, two Martello Towers were built to defend Longhope Sound, Hoy, in Orkney, together with a new battery at Hackness. These were not completed until after the peace with France in 1815.

The round towers built in the Channel Islands, resembling the English and Irish Martello Towers, were among the earliest to be built in Britain, construction starting in the late eighteenth century as a response to the French threats of 1779. They were smaller and differed in design from other Martello Towers. The fifteen towers built on Guernsey were slightly smaller than the twenty-two built on Jersey, mounting just the small 12 pounder carronade. They remained active until the middle of the nineteenth century, forming part of the island's defences against nearby France. Their military life was extended in the Second World War when the German occupiers

Leith Tower, Edinburgh: originally conceived in 1807 to protect the harbour at Leith, this tower was not completed until thirty years later.

of the islands used a number for military purposes, for example that at Saumurez, which supported a concrete four-storey observation post.

Other, larger and detached towers (although not true Martello Towers) were built in the mid nineteenth century at Pembroke Dock, Sheerness (the Spit of Grain Tower), and at Brehon, Guernsey. That at Sheerness was built to improve the Medway defences. Remaining in use into the twentieth century, it was rearmed with

Pembroke Dock Gun Towers, Pembrokeshire: the north-eastern of the two towers built in the middle of the nineteenth century, its exterior of high-quality cut stone. Three guns were mounted on its roof, together with internal casemated guns.

Pembroke Dock Gun Towers, Pembrokeshire: the south-western tower, of a more angular design than that of its neighbour.

4.7 inch (119 mm) quick-firing guns in the First World War, and in the Second World War with the twin 6 pounder anti-motor-torpedo-boat gun, the tower's base also providing a convenient attachment point for the Medway boom defence. Brehon had the luxury of latrines and was armed with 68 pounder and 10 inch (254 mm) shell guns; it was built as part of the rearming of the Channel Islands in response to the threat from the French port of Cherbourg in the middle of the nineteenth century. In 1940 it was adapted by the Germans to mount light anti-aircraft guns. Martello-like towers were also built on Bermuda, Mauritius and in South Africa. By the mid nineteenth century these final, larger towers were becoming, with the advent of the explosive shell and rifled cannon, as obsolete as contemporary masonry fortresses.

The disarming of the towers began as early as 1818. Of the seventy-four built in Kent and Sussex only twenty-six remain. The east-coast towers have fared better, eighteen out of the twenty-nine surviving. Along the south coast the sea has been

Pembroke Dock Gun Towers, Pembrokeshire: the interior of the smaller, south-western tower, showing an original kitchen range.

the biggest enemy of the towers; by the mid nineteenth century eight were already lost. One unusual side effect of the presence of the manned towers was a reduction in smuggling, especially following the building of the Royal Military Canal. Some towers were converted for use by the coastguard service for coast watching, while others housed the crews of adjacent semaphore signal stations, an efficient anti-invasion signalling system that was introduced in the south and east of England in the late eighteenth century. Some upgrading of arms took place, with guns of 32 or 68 pounder calibres replacing the earlier guns, although along the east coast all but five towers remained unarmed. The last tower to be used for its original intended purpose was Tower N, which, with a new 9 inch (229 mm) rifled muzzle-loading gun battery nearby, and together with Landguard Fort and Shotley Battery, formed part of the upgraded Harwich defences well into the late nineteenth century. This tower, in fitting with its continued use, was provided with a winched access drawbridge. Two south-coast towers were used by the War Department in 1860 for artillery experiments: two hundred rounds from new rifled guns were required to demolish the thinner rear wall, but a smooth-bore gun firing a similar number of shots at the other tower failed to make any significant impression. A small number of towers were also destroyed with the aid of the new guncotton explosive, one requiring 200 pounds (91 kg) of explosive to do the job, perhaps a fitting compliment to the efficiency and strength of the original design.

There were no major European wars affecting Britain between 1815 and 1853, and the country had been able to maintain a balance of power by virtue of her powerful navy, although, as usual, there were a number of invasion scares. However, this naval superiority was perhaps more potential than actual: for reasons of economy much of the navy had been laid up during the period. Future and increasing overseas commitments would also gradually drain the strength of the pool for Channel protection. France, on the other hand, still possessed the largest army in western Europe, and also the only navy capable of challenging British supremacy in the English Channel. A modest degree of fortress building and upgrading did take place

Fort Perch Rock, Wirral, Cheshire: one of the few fortifications built in the 1820s, it supported a gun battery to protect the mouth of the Mersey and the expanding port of Liverpool. The structure on the top of the left-hand tower is a Second World War battery-observation post.

during this period. In addition to the regular fear of a French invasion there was the countrywide risk of attacks on the country's ports and shipping by commerce raiders. In the light of this risk, and facing the expanding west-coast of Liverpool across the Mersey, a new battery was built at Fort Perch Rock in the 1820s, the site being located on a rocky outcrop in the mouth of the river.

The Industrial Revolution makes an impact

In the first half of the nineteenth century the world's navies were still largely dependent on sail power, although the first steam-driven ships had begun to appear in numbers after the beginning of the century. The early paddle-propelled warships had limited gun space and their paddles were considered to be extremely vulnerable to cannon fire. In 1837 the French navy adopted the shell gun, with Britain following suit the year after. The greater range, hitting power and accuracy of this new generation of naval gun meant that engagements could now be undertaken at greater distances, and this, of course, included attacks on coastal fortifications. In 1852 HMS *Agamemnon*, the first British steam-driven screw ship, was launched. The combination of screw, steam power and shell gun offered the potential for much greater speed, manoeuvrability and firepower, and this new breed of warship began to dominate the seas. The launch of the armoured warship *La Gloire*, armed with rifled muzzle-loading guns, in 1858 gave the French a temporary lead, to be followed in 1859 by the similarly armoured warship HMS *Warrior*, fitted with smooth-bores and one of the new Armstrong 7 inch (178 mm) breach-loading guns. The French and British dockyards were now in a technological race, making them more than ever a target for attack.

Many of the technological innovations of the nineteenth century had an impact upon the design and construction of fortifications. The construction of buildings using iron girders had begun, and also emerging were improvements in waterproofing,

Newhaven Fort, East Sussex: the entrance with, to the right, the start of the concrete revetment of the ditch. A Second World War pillbox sits above the gateway, which was protected by musket holes.

lighting, drainage, and hydraulic and mechanical lifting devices. The most far-reaching development, however, was the discovery of hydraulic cement and its gradual introduction into fortress construction. Up to the middle of the nineteenth century military construction had used only brick and stone, but from the 1860s concrete started to make significant inroads into building and engineering works. It was to be used extensively in the waterproofing of brick casemates, arches and floors, in the construction of foundations, in the revetment of ditches, and in the shellproofing of casemates against plunging fire.

The first location at which concrete was used in large quantities was Newhaven Fort in Sussex, where, in 1865, it revetted the ditch walls. By using this new material a considerable saving was made in cost and time over the use of brick and stone. From the 1870s concrete was also used to form the pits for the new Moncrieff disappearing gun carriage and for the shaping of the sloping aprons of the gun pits. The Chatham Ring, a system of fortifications proposed by the 1860 report of the Royal Commission, used both brick and concrete, the latter being increasingly used. New coastal fortifications could also take advantage of the plentiful supplies of local gravel for making the concrete. The material would also come into its own in the building of caponiers, counterscarp galleries, fort gateways and the aprons, gun pits and magazines of the new coastal batteries appearing at the end of the century. Tests had shown that, although a shell penetrated twice as far into concrete as into granite, the masonry shattered and splintered lethally and the masonry courses moved, whereas concrete stayed relatively intact, absorbing damage around the missile's path. By the end of the century the continental powers would also use concrete increasingly in the construction of their new fortresses, burying barracks and artillery casemates beneath carapaces of concrete and soil.

While the theory and practice of fortification had undergone important developments in the first half of the nineteenth century, artillery had also experienced change. The guns in this period were similar to but larger than those that had armed Henry VIII's fortifications, but they had become more reliable and accurate. At the turn of the nineteenth century, for example, the main armament on Drake's Island at Plymouth was the 32 pounder smooth-bore muzzle-loader, with 42 pounders at the Royal Citadel – some of the largest calibres in the kingdom at that time. The guns still fired solid, cast-iron balls with a high muzzle velocity, but the poor aerodynamic shape of the shot limited their accuracy. The effective range of these early-nineteenth-century guns was about 2000 yards (1829 metres), or more at 5 degrees of elevation, their extreme practical range being just over 3000 yards (2743 metres): this was not a significant advance on the performance of Tudor artillery.

Earlier gun batteries had had considerable difficulty in engaging moving targets, as the iron-wheeled land garrison gun carriage was traversed only with difficulty, using ropes or long wooden hand spikes as levers. In the late eighteenth century came the gradual introduction of traversing carriages with wheels running on arced iron rails. The aiming of the guns was by reference to graduations marked on the breech ring, target acquisition being via a notch on the muzzle. Tangent sights, offering more accuracy and fitted to the top of the breech, came into use later in the nineteenth century, with ranges being set on a vertical scale. Against larger targets, for example warships, the range was kept short to ensure maximum hitting power from the shot. Initially ignited by a linstock, the powder charges of guns would later be ignited by a flintlock, then, with the appearance of breech-loading artillery, by a cartridge initiated by pulling on a lanyard. Apart from solid shot, other forms of projectile were used. Chain shot was useful for the cutting of rigging, while grape and case shot were devastating against advancing troops, the latter being supplied for guns in flank positions for the clearing of ditches and curtain walls.

From the 1720s onwards howitzers began to appear, using exploding shells with primitive fuses, a lighter charge being used in the barrel so as not to burst the shell. Howitzers had the advantage of being able to deliver shells over an enemy's walls or on to the decks of his ships. The earlier mortars were still in service and with development came more reliable fuses, the mortar being much used at the siege of Sebastopol in the Crimean War. Of limited accuracy, they were effective only against larger targets, but their bombs could penetrate roofs in their near-vertical descent and explode internally with devastating effect. During the Napoleonic Wars 10 inch (254 mm) and 13 inch (330 mm) mortars, for example, were emplaced at Plymouth at the Citadel, at Mount Wise and on Drake's Island.

At the end of the eighteenth century artillery was being increasingly accommodated in casemates (for example at Fort Cumberland), which, in addition to being more efficient for the close defence of the work, had the advantage of giving protection against the plunging fire of mortars and howitzers. The disadvantages of casemated guns were their confined nature, the localised blast effect when the guns were fired, the choking powder smoke, and their limited field of fire in comparison with guns mounted on a terreplein. However, those fortifications close to the coast had the added advantage that the casemates protected the gun crews from the sharpshooters located in a warship's rigging, as well as against the warship's case shot and sea service mortars that began to appear from the 1860s.

These developments were minor in comparison with the effect on the design of fortifications of the introduction in the middle of the nineteenth century of the new generation of rifled guns, breech-loading or muzzle-loading and firing explosive shells propelled by new, bagged charges. The new rifled breech-loading artillery, initially troubled by technical defects, trebled the range of existing guns and gave improved accuracy and rates of fire, while the heavier and bulkier rifled muzzle-loaders resulted in guns of much greater calibre and penetrative power. These latter guns were simpler to manufacture than the breech-loading gun, were more reliable and were capable of more rapid development. On the other hand, they were slow to load. The earliest rifled guns had three spiral grooves in the barrel that engaged with three studs on the side of the newly invented Palliser shell: the spin imparted by the grooves greatly increased the accuracy of the aerodynamic projectile. The effect of

Fort Brockhurst, Gosport, Hampshire: a 9 inch (229 mm) rifled muzzle-loading gun in a casemate. The large inclined carriage can be seen, to be replaced in the late nineteenth century by neater, hydraulic recoil systems.

explosive shells, greater ranges and penetrative power pointed to the need for thicker walls and parapets, smaller embrasures, yet lower profiles, together with bombproof magazines and barracks proof against the direct or plunging fire of the new guns.

In the 1860s Captain Alexander Moncrieff had proposed a new, counterbalanced gun carriage. On firing, the gun recoiled behind the parapet, enabling reloading to take place under cover, the gun then returning briefly to its firing position by means of counterweights. Only a small number of guns of this design were issued in 1871, but the idea found favour and in 1877 an improved and more successful design was produced. The disappearing-carriage design was refined yet further in the 1880s, leading eventually to the Elswick hydro-pneumatic mounting married to the new and highly successful 6 inch (152 mm) breech-loading Armstrong coast-defence gun, this combination appearing in a number of late-nineteenth-century British fortifications. In the trials in 1885 at Portland involving HMS *Hercules*, pitted against 6 inch (152 mm) coastal guns on disappearing carriages, the warship had been unable to hit the guns – a proof of the worth of the new carriage. The complicated and expensive hydro-pneumatic mounting had a relatively short life, however, being superseded by the new generation of low-profile coast artillery batteries, their shells propelled by the newly invented smokeless and more powerful explosive charges such as cordite, which appeared at the end of the nineteenth century.

7

'Palmerston's Follies' and a defence scheme for London

In 1842 the Duke of Wellington had advocated better land defences in order to reduce the burden on the army and the navy. He felt that the army would be unable adequately to protect all of Britain's major ports and dockyards, especially against a surprise attack. From 1846 onwards fears were expressed, especially by the Foreign Secretary Lord Palmerston, that the French might rush a large army across the Channel in their new steamships. Despite these concerns, only moderate progress was made in the way of new works during this period.

The move away from the bastioned trace had, however, begun in the 1840s with the building of the new Shornemead fort in Kent, built in the polygonal style of Montalembert between 1848 and 1852. This design was not entirely new to Britain: in 1779 a line of four-sided irregularly shaped earthwork redoubts had been built on the Maker Heights at Plymouth, largely because the uneven nature of the ground made the current bastioned trace unsuitable. In 1810, during the Peninsular War, similar works of fortification, known as the Lines of Torres Vedras, had been built by the British in Spain. As at Maker Heights, they were adapted to the lie of the land and, despite not being connected to each other by ramparts and ditches, were effective against the weakened French forces. Shornemead also possessed caponiers and bombproof vaults, and, in keeping with Montalembert's principles, the rampart space was devoted solely to offensive firepower. Three sides faced the Thames, these containing the offensive artillery, while the remaining two (landward) sides contained barrack accommodation.

There was further fear of invasion in 1851–2, which again highlighted the inadequacies of the coastal defences and spurred the Government to consider funding

Fort Tourgis, Alderney: one of a number of batteries and fortified barracks built by Jervois in the 1850s.

more up-to-date works. Three areas of the country were identified as needing such works: Milford Haven, the western approaches to Portsmouth, and the island of Alderney. The last of these had been identified in 1844 by the Admiralty as one of a number of refuges to be established in response to the growth of the fortified port of Cherbourg. The majority of the thirteen new fortifications on Alderney were designed by Captain Jervois, later to be Deputy Director of Works for Fortifications, while overall planning was in the hands of his superior, General Burgoyne, the Inspector General. The fortifications were designed to hold batteries and also to provide for the local protection of landing-places by the provision of attached infantry blockhouses, many of the works having distinctly medieval touches – for example, round towers. At Milford Haven defensible, bastioned barracks were built above the docks in 1841. The new Milford Haven works of the 1850s were pushed forward and into the haven: Stack Rock was occupied in 1850 and Thorn Island in 1852, and four years later Dale Fort and West Blockhouse were built. At Portsmouth it was apparent that there were weaknesses in the western landward and seaborne approaches. The chief defence had for long been Hurst Castle, but this would be supplemented by works on the Isle of Wight: the angular brick Fort Albert and Fort Victoria, the latter a redan-shaped artillery work with open casemates at the water's edge. Both of these works would soon be rendered obsolete with the development of rifled cannon. On the landward approaches to Portsmouth two new polygonal works were started in 1852 across the Gosport peninsula: Fort Gomer and Fort Elson.

Between 1854 and 1856, despite rivalries and alarms caused by French naval developments, the British and French were briefly allies against Russia in the Crimean War. In this conflict the French used floating, iron-armoured batteries and had attacked Fort Kinburn: to the Russians' alarm their return fire failed to penetrate the French

St Catherine's Castle, Cornwall: a small, two-gun centre-pivot battery of 1855 below the Henrician blockhouse overlooking Polruan Harbour. Polruan and Fowey both possessed early artillery blockhouses, that at Polruan being visible on the headland facing the castle. In the Second World War a quick-firing battery was also built on the site.

ships. The Royal Navy, on the other hand, was waging a long and ineffectual campaign against the port of Kronstadt, itself defended by strong, casemated forts and batteries equipped with modern guns. The actions in the war, Kinburn excepted, reinforced the belief that modern coast defences could still resist bombardment from the sea, although it was accepted that they would remain vulnerable to artillery batteries landed by the enemy navy.

By the end of the Crimean War in 1856 the British army had become overstretched, the majority of its resources being overseas. France had a conscript army and was capable of putting four times as many troops into the field, despite Britain's part-time militias and volunteers. There were clearly not enough regular troops to man the home defences and to repel an invasion. In 1858 suspicions over French intentions increased with the launching of the armoured warship *La Gloire*, which had the potential to render British coastal batteries obsolete, together with the continued development of the great French naval harbour of Cherbourg.

The rising strategic importance of Sussex, and Shoreham harbour in particular, together with the growing alarm about the intentions of Louis Napoleon, led to the building of two similarly designed fortifications at Littlehampton and Shoreham in the 1850s. Both were in the shape of a straight-sided crescent with a Carnot wall in their ditches and mounting 68 pounder guns, but they differed in that the one at Shoreham was provided with a single caponier. Their design and situation were not judged a success: that at Shoreham was built on shingle, which if hit by round shot would have acted like shrapnel. In 1858 there was a further review of the fortifications of the ports of Plymouth, Portsmouth and Milford Haven, and the fortification of the Gosport Peninsula was finally completed by the building of Forts Grange, Rowner and Brockhurst, the last of these finished in 1863. At Plymouth the only forward positions had been the obsolete batteries at Picklecombe and Staddon Point. New works were now proposed at Tregantle and Scraesdon, along with some new batteries, as well as additional detached works north and north-west of Plymouth. At Milford Haven the object was the prevention not just of the destruction of the docks but also of their use as an anchorage by an enemy. Two lines of defence were

Fort Brockhurst, Gosport, Hampshire: model showing the keep, corner caponiers and the ravelin in front of the entrance.

Fort Brockhurst, Gosport, Hampshire: a view of the exterior of the fort with barrack accommodation in the foreground and the circular keep beyond.

Fort Brockhurst, Gosport, Hampshire: the detached keep from across its moat, showing the entrance protected by tall caponiers.

proposed behind the forts of West Blockhouse, Dale and Thorn Island. The first consisted of the strengthened Stack Rock along with batteries at Chapel Bay and South Hook Point. The second line consisted of Fort Hubberston and Popton Fort, and a defensible barracks behind each was proposed. At three of these pre-1860s works – Forts Brockhurst, Tregantle and Popton – Jervois had built keeps, designed to enable a small number of men to defend both the interiors and the approaches to the gorges of the forts. His post-1860 works would be less elaborate, although still with an emphasis on gorge and ditch protection.

Despite the co-operation between Britain and France in the Crimean War, there was mounting distrust between the two governments. In addition to naval rivalry, Britain felt challenged by her neighbour's construction of the Suez Canal. On the other hand, Britain had a more developed economy, increasingly based on heavy industry. The Orsini plot to assassinate Napoleon III had been hatched in Britain, and so there was mutual suspicion and animosity.

In June 1859 Lord Palmerston became Prime Minister and in August a Royal Commission was appointed in the light of a fear that the French would mount an attack paralysing Britain's principal arsenals and naval dockyards. The Commission was asked to 'consider the best means of rendering these dockyards defensible within as short a time as possible in order to be prepared for any sudden emergency and how they can be put in the most complete state of defence by permanent fortifications'. The navy had always been relied upon as the first line of defence, but now, with increasing overseas commitments, it could not be depended upon entirely to keep Britain free from invasion. Only fifty years earlier a leading politician had said 'I don't say the enemy can't come, but he cannot come by sea'. Now the Government was not so confident. Fortification was again felt to be the key to national security, but the Government's demand was that it had to be economical in terms of both money and manpower.

The background to the setting up of the Royal Commission had been, first, the introduction in 1858 of the Armstrong rifled breech-loading gun with a range of 8000 yards (7315 metres), double that of contemporary artillery. It was assumed that other countries would soon follow suit. The implication was that most of Britain's fixed defences were now obsolete and her naval installations were open to attack from land and sea. Second, the onset of the ironclad warship (*La Gloire*) had generated a feeling that France was not only equal to Britain but was likely to overtake her in warship design and production. Britain, with her extensive overseas possessions, was in a weaker position than France, which could afford to keep more warships on home station and was therefore potentially in a position to dominate the Channel and rapidly mount an invasion.

The Commission had concentrated on the protection of the royal dockyards and naval bases, especially against the possibility of landings in their rear areas, this being considered to be the most likely means of attack, particularly for those areas situated by the English Channel. The Commission's remit also included an examination of the plans of the works that were already in progress at Portsmouth (including the Isle of Wight and Spithead), Plymouth, Portland, Pembroke Dock, Dover, Chatham and the Medway. In February 1860 it made its recommendations to Parliament. As a result of the Commission's report seventy-six new works of fortification, at an initial estimated cost of almost £12 million, would be built. The proposals met with strong opposition; one body of military thought, known as the 'Blue Water School', felt that there was no need for expensive fixed defences as any threat of invasion could still be met by the Royal Navy. Further opposition came from the Chancellor, Gladstone, and the work was eventually agreed only on the basis of annual loans.

The majority of the works were shore batteries, with some powerful curved, casemated batteries being built near sea level, for example those at Hurst Castle, Hampshire, and at Bovisand, Plymouth. Their design was influenced by experiences in the sieges of the Crimean War in which curved and casemated batteries had appeared impervious to naval gunfire. Their role was to block the sea approaches to naval harbours, dockyards and installations. As wide an arc of fire as possible was felt to be desirable, together with double tiers of guns, although in the event only two works received these: Picklecombe Fort at Plymouth and Garrison Point at Sheerness in Kent. The casemated muzzle-loading guns were slow to load and traverse, hence the need for a large number of guns to be installed to follow an enemy's ships. The rifled muzzle-loader could pierce the sides of ironclads with horizontal fire and therefore, unlike the earlier smooth-bore guns whose shot was designed to land on decks, the elevation of coastal batteries was not material. Magazines were safely situated under the batteries, ammunition being raised on davits from below the casemates, and shells were moved on trolleys, the heavier shells being raised to the guns' muzzles by block and tackle. There was separate storage and movement of shells and bagged charges (called 'cartridges'), together with an emphasis on remote and safe lighting in the magazines.

Where the approaches to ports and harbours were too wide to be adequately swept by converging battery fire a number of armoured sea forts were proposed and built, of iron and concrete, at Portsmouth, Plymouth, Portland and Milford Haven. To prevent a landward attack, lines of forts were recommended to cover such approaches. These were to be polygonal in shape, of four to seven sides, and giving supporting fire to the other forts in the line. The prevention of a surprise attack on a fort was to be achieved by a system of all-round defence, the deep and narrow ditches of the forts being covered by the fire from rifles and light artillery pieces. These would be positioned in ditch caponiers and counterscarp galleries set in the outer sections of the ditches. The advantage of the galleries was that they could maintain the defence of the ditch even if the caponiers had been destroyed by plunging howitzer or mortar fire.

Huge numbers of guns were required for the new forts, but the navy had a prior call on the new rifled breech- and muzzle-loading guns. Only by the 1880s were sufficient numbers of the more modern guns made available, obsolete guns having to be used in the meantime. Coastal defence batteries were temporarily armed with the last generation of the smooth-bore guns of the 1840s. In casemated batteries these were replaced by 9 inch (229 mm) and 10 inch (254 mm) rifled muzzle-loaders firing 250 pound and 400 pound shells respectively, these being capable of penetrating 11 inches (279 mm) and 14 inches (356 mm) of iron plate.

At the time of the Crimean War Britain had had a volunteer army of 135,000 men, approximately half of these being stationed at home. The Royal Commission estimated that, for example, Plymouth would require a wartime garrison of over ten thousand men, many of these recruited from local levies, or being moved into place from elsewhere by the new railway system. However, the volunteers, including the Corps of Artillery, were not liable for military service until an invasion had actually begun! The militias and the volunteers were quite independent and under no single overall control, the militia being officered by country gentlemen with little military training. The Royal Commission works were not, in any event, universally popular among the military, being felt to be the 'enemy of artillery' as so much time was absorbed by the soldiers in the arming or rearming of the forts and batteries, with little opportunity for training to take place.

Used in the American Civil War of 1861–5, the new rifled guns gave greater accuracy, range and penetration: this was shown by their efficient destruction of Fort Pulaski. It also emphasised the absolute need for 'bombproofs' – casemated barracks, magazines and artillery positions. A covering of 6 feet (1.8 metres) or more of earth and rubble above the casemate was held to be proof, at that time, against plunging mortar bombs or howitzer shells. The lessons learned in the American Civil War were analysed and incorporated into the Royal Commission works, sometimes during the course of their construction. New armoured shields of iron and teak to protect the embrasures of the casemates were now introduced, although this was often delayed, and internal rope mantlets protected the gun crews from bullets and splinters. The

Civil War had also demonstrated that fewer guns, separated by protective earth traverses, were more effective than many guns in entirely open positions.

By 1885 the land forts were in varying stages of full armament, although all coastal fortifications were by then fully armed. The Moncrieff disappearing carriage, introduced later in the century, helped to reduce considerably the profile of the heavy ordnance mounted on the terrepleins of the new forts. Quick-firing guns began to be emplaced to protect naval installations and underwater (submarine) minefields were introduced in the 1880s against the new fast motor torpedo boats and gunboats. The new generation of breech-loading coastal defence guns was also under development at this time. By 1893 the land forts were more or less fully armed, but from this time guns started to be removed from the casemated coast batteries as the coastal defence layout became modernised. In their place would be a new generation of cheaper-to-construct, low-profile batteries with open positions mounting the new 6 inch (152 mm) and 9.2 inch (234 mm) breech-loading guns.

Once the report of the Commission had been agreed by Parliament in 1860 the intention was that the work would start immediately, although it was realised that there would be a delay in producing all of the new armaments for the forts and batteries. It would be the largest scheme of national fortification to date. Men of considerable influence were involved, for example General Burgoyne and Major Jervois RE (who would soon become Secretary to the Royal Commission). Burgoyne had had long experience in the art of fortification and recognised the need for all-round defence. Jervois, as we have seen, had been active in the previous decade at Alderney, Plymouth, Portsmouth and Milford Haven. The Defence Committee was in charge of its execution and Jervois superintended the engineer officers who were drawing up the designs for the individual works. At each location the garrison strength was laid down first (the system of fortifications had been recommended to Parliament as being economical in manpower), and detailed plans for the actual layout of the fortifications followed later. In 1862 Jervois was appointed Deputy Director of Works for Fortification and was now in a position to supervise and influence the works more adequately. His appointment also led to some simplification in the range of coast artillery guns to be installed. In addition he held to the view that casemated coastal batteries were desirable where there was a risk of coastal artillery being subject to counter-battery fire from the sea. The new Royal Commission coastal batteries at Plymouth, for example, were casemated. The landward works were to be mutually supporting, their size varying with the nature of the ground and their complement of guns. The polygonal trace was considered the most appropriate, with an obtuse angle to the enemy's front, and with converging fire, the object being to cover all of the ground not covered by another work. The bastioned trace was now largely out of fashion. Ramparts became lower and lay behind a glacis and deep ditches, and to avoid enfilade fire the guns on the terreplein were protected by traverses or were in Haxo surface casemates.

In 1868 a further parliamentary commission looked into the progress of the 1860 works. Although many deviations from the original plans were revealed, the coastal defences of the Plymouth area were found to have been largely completed in accordance with the original specifications. Of concern was the slow rate of fire of the rifled muzzle-loaders against faster-moving targets; individual firing rates were between one and two and a half rounds per minute, depending on the type of gun. In the following years heavier-calibre guns became more widely available, for example the 64 pounder or larger: by 1872 the Defence Committee was recommending that all existing guns be replaced with these heavier guns. But they were much more costly than the smooth-bores on which the original 1860 estimates had been based. It appears that even at this stage some forts still had no guns, and some magazines, especially those built by civilian contractors, were judged to be insufficiently bombproof.

In 1875 the Defence Committee made detailed recommendations for the land defences, the 7 inch (178 mm) rifled breech-loader and the 64 pounder rifled muzzle-loader now being advocated as the optimum armament for the works. The 8 inch (203 mm) howitzer was intended to replace the mortars fitted into vaulted pits at such works as Fort Nelson on Portsdown Hill, and the 32 pounder smooth-bores were to act as flanking guns. By 1880 the Inspector General of Fortifications felt that the works were in a satisfactory state, even in the light of recent artillery advances. But not all of the work was complete. The 1860 timetable had been hopelessly optimistic and had also been adversely affected by the need for modifications, such as the supply of armoured covers for casemates, as a result of recent developments in artillery. However, in 1871 the defeat of France in her war with Prussia largely removed for Britain the threat from across the Channel for the foreseeable future, and the delays, although regrettable, were now becoming less relevant. Both France and Prussia, and soon the new Germany, would invest vast sums of money in fortifications similar to those of the Royal Commission to protect their new borders and their important cities. The British forts, on their completion, had been well regarded by continental engineers such as the Belgian General Brialmont, who referred to their construction as 'a triumph'.

AREAS AFFECTED BY THE ROYAL COMMISSION'S PROPOSALS
Plymouth
The principal historic dockyards were those at Portsmouth, Plymouth and Chatham. Plymouth was Britain's second-greatest naval arsenal and dock for men-of-war: it was also important to the defence of this somewhat geographically isolated part of the West Country. Because of its splendid harbour, the city had received early artillery fortifications, including those built by Henry VIII, together with a number of other early artillery blockhouses such as those surviving at Firestone Bay and Mount Edgcumbe. A star-shaped fort on the Hoe was completed in 1596 after earlier Armada scares. The city played only a minor part in the English Civil War although after the conflict the Commonwealth built a circular artillery tower at Mount Batten,

Crownhill Fort, Plymouth: the elaborate entrance, modelled on a Norman church doorway.

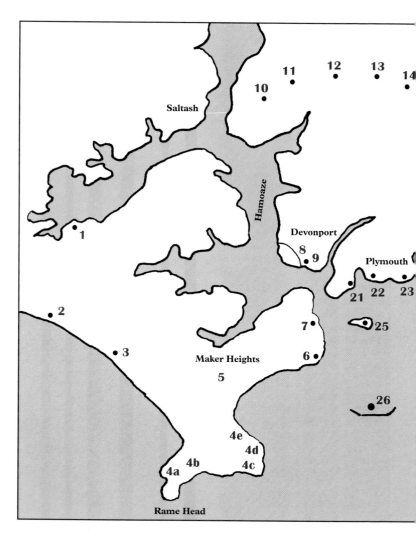

and after the Restoration the building of the Citadel was begun to a design by de Gomme. Batteries were built on Drake's Island at the time of the Seven Years War of 1756–63, and in 1784 the innovative five redoubts were built at Maker. By the end of the Napoleonic Wars Plymouth had become one of the largest industrial complexes in Britain. The continuing possibility of invasion by France, together with the strategic importance of the city and its dockyards, led to a complex system of fortification being developed in the nineteenth century, reflecting the intricate topography of the area.

In 1844 the Committee on the Harbour Defences of Plymouth recommended the construction of new batteries at Picklecombe and Staddon Point (Bovisand) to cover either side of the new Cattewater breakwater. The Prince of Wales Redoubt at Eastern King was also built at this time, the Citadel was rearmed, and in 1853 the Devonport Lines were modernised. However, these works were now becoming obsolete in the face of the armoured warship. In 1860 the Royal Commission's proposals for Plymouth resulted in the completion of six new coast batteries, together

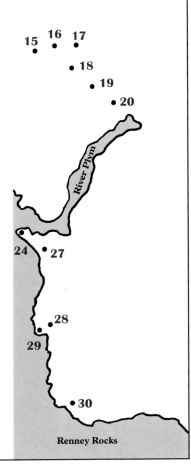

The defences of Plymouth (after Woodward, 1998, and Saunders, 1989).

1. Screasden Fort
2. Tregantle Fort
3. Whitesand Bay Battery
4a. Polhawn Battery
4b. Rame Church Battery
4c. Penlee Point Battery
4d. Pier Cellars Battery
4e. Cawsand Battery
5. Maker Heights Redoubts
6. Picklecombe Fort
7. Garden Battery
8. Devonport Lines
9. Mount Wise Redoubt
10. Ernesettle Fort
11. Agaton Fort
12. Knowles Battery
13. Woodland Fort
14. Crownhill Fort
15. Bowden Fort
16. Egg Buckland Keep
17. Forder Battery
18. Austin Fort
19. Fort Efford
20. Laira Battery
21. Western King Battery and Tower
22. Firestone Bay Tower
23. Plymouth Citadel
24. Mount Batten Tower
25. Drake's Island Battery
26. Breakwater Fort
27. Fort Stamford
28. Fort Staddon
29. Fort Bovisand
30. Renney Battery

with Breakwater Fort and a ring of eighteen land forts based on three powerful forts at Staddon, Crownhill and Tregantle. The fortifications would accommodate seven thousand men, although this figure could be increased to fifteen thousand at the time of any emergency. Shortly after the recommendations of the Commission had been announced it was realised that the open-fronted granite casemated batteries were now too vulnerable, not only to the new generation of rifled guns but also to musket fire from landing parties. Armour-plating trials of shields had been carried out at Shoeburyness in Essex with wrought-iron plates combined with a teak or iron concrete sandwich. Trials of the shields were also carried out at the new battery at Picklecombe. The decision was now made to cover or replace the recessed embrasures of granite in the new coastal batteries with iron shields. But progress was slow and it was only in 1873 that all of the huge Picklecombe shields, covering two tiers of guns, were in position.

A progress report was prepared in 1867 and it was noted that the Plymouth work had moved ahead quickly. The massive granite casemated Picklecombe, with provision for forty-two guns, and Staddon Point (Bovisand) were, however, only half complete. A similar situation applied to the new battery on Drake's Island. These three works were designed for the 68 pounder smooth-bore gun, although by 1864 this weapon had become obsolete and was replaced by the 9 inch (229 mm) and 10 inch (254 mm) rifled muzzle-loader. The smallest battery (Garden) was almost complete, the extensions to the batteries at Eastern and Western Kings were also complete, Cawsand Battery was finished, and work on Breakwater Fort was progressing. The last of these was the subject of many modifications, its final configuration being of two floors with the magazines on the lower storey and thirty-three guns on the upper, the floors being serviced by a central lift. Its walls were of four thicknesses of 5 inch (127 mm) plate separated by a concrete filling. Tregantle was nearly complete, as was Scraesdon. Stamford Fort and Brownhill Battery were connected by a military road and were protected by a deep ditch and high rampart.

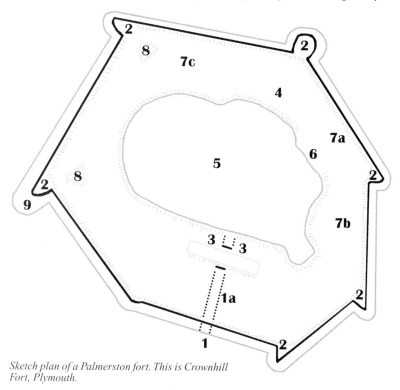

Sketch plan of a Palmerston fort. This is Crownhill Fort, Plymouth.

1. *Entrance to fort via bridge and tunnel beneath ramparts (1a)*
2. *Caponiers*
3. *Officers' quarters (under ramparts)*
4. *Magazine (under ramparts)*
5. *Courtyard*
6. *Soldiers' quarters (under ramparts)*
7a. *Moncrieff and pivot gun positions*
7b. *Double Haxo casemate*
7c. *Gun emplacements (further)*
8. *Mortar pits*
9. *Ditch*

Crownhill Fort, Plymouth: gun drill on a 7 inch (178 mm) rifled breech-loading gun on a Moncrieff disappearing carriage in its emplacement.

The Saltash defences were never progressed, however, leaving a significant gap to the north-west of the city.

Captain du Cane was the principal engineer at Plymouth, designing and skilfully siting the north-easterly and Staddon defences to cover hilly country and steep valleys with guns and mortars. In the works at Portsmouth it had proved relatively easy to dig ditches in the softer chalk rock, brick was used, and there was more of a commonality in the designs. At Plymouth, however, the hard rock, laboriously dug out to make ditches, was worked into masonry, and because of the broken nature of the ground each fort was to be to a different design. The work was done by civilian contractors and by soldiers of the Royal Engineers. Itinerant labourers provided the muscle power, these having only recently been employed building the new Great Western Railway line, living in temporary hutted or tented camps.

General Todleben, the Russian military engineer and stout defender of Sebastopol, a former enemy, was invited during the

Tregantle Fort, Plymouth: the glacis (left), ditch and eastern wall with one of the caponiers for the flanking of the ditch.

71

Tregantle Fort, Plymouth: the keep and interior of the fort. Haxo casemates can be seen on the right-hand parapet.

construction of Plymouth's defences to visit and comment upon them. He approved in 1864 of the detached batteries and of the massive Tregantle Fort's semicircular casemated and loopholed keep as a place of last resort, although the latter had been extremely costly to build. Todleben would have preferred more of the very strong forts such as Tregantle, the key to the western defences. He thought that Crownhill Fort was 'magnificent', being the keystone of the Devonport land defences, with its ramparts concealed from the north, with developed caponiers, bombproofed casemates and *chemins des rondes*, and being less than half the cost of Tregantle. Overall, he preferred the defences of Plymouth to those of Portsmouth because they presented a more complete girdle. Crownhill Fort was the key to the north-eastern land defences, which included four batteries and the forts of Efford, Austin, Egg Buckland, Bowden, Woodland and Agaton. It was the last of the Plymouth forts to be completed, its ditches and seven wall faces covered by one double and five single caponiers for muskets or cannon firing case shot. It had bombproofed accommodation and magazines, as well as sunken mortar positions. The scarp wall had rifle slits running around the fort. Its armament in the 1870s consisted of the 7 inch (177 mm) rifled breech-loaders in Moncrieff, casemated or open positions, 64 pounder rifled muzzle-loaders *en barbette*, and fourteen 32 pounder smooth-bores converted to breech-loaders for the sweeping of the ditches with case shot.

Crownhill Fort, occupying 16 acres (6.5 hectares), had been completed in 1872 for the relatively low figure of £76,000. It was one of only two 'typical forts' (the other being Fort Widley at Portsmouth) to have its complete peacetime armament in place in the 1880s. In the same period improvements occurred in the design of magazines: no longer would gunpowder be stored loose in wooden barrels but it would now be in ready-to-use cartridges, efficiently and safely stored in the magazines. The fort possesses a unique countermining gallery. Often found on continental fortifications, the gallery ran from the fort and around the hillside surrounding it. The gallery was designed to locate and intercept any enemy attempts to mine the fort. Crownhill Fort, now open to the public, presents, too, an insight into the life of the Victorian soldier. Two unlit and unheated cells were positioned by the guardhouse for soldiers guilty of minor breaches of discipline: these might have been common given that, until the reforms of 1900, over twenty men would eat, sleep and socialise in each barrack room.

Fort Bovisand, Plymouth: a ditch (to the left) protects Staddon Point Battery A (middle ground) and Fort Bovisand, whose curved casemates can be seen near the water's edge. Two director towers for a Second World War 6 pounder quick-firing battery can be seen on the roof of the casemates. The structure in the foreground is a searchlight directing post.

The Staddon Heights defences on the east side of the harbour had first been proposed by Jervois in 1858, these being designed to deny the Heights, which overlooked parts of the city, and certain of its harbours and channels, to an enemy. The land defences consisted of two forts, Stamford and Staddon, together with three batteries, to form an integrated system. The seaward defences consisted of the 1844 battery, later to be used as accommodation only, and the powerful curved and casemated Fort Bovisand Battery. The sea fort, Breakwater Fort, was built to control access to the harbour mouth but was completed in 1880 only with difficulty after cracks had developed in its sides.

The defences of Plymouth would be further strengthened after the report of the 1887 Stanhope Committee identified urgent requirements: a new threat to shipping had emerged in the form of the fast motor torpedo boat. As a result new batteries, such as that at Fort Bovisand with its three pairs of Hotchkiss 6 pounder quick-firing guns, and searchlight positions were built. At the beginning of the twentieth century several new batteries were erected for harbour defence, including the 9.2 inch (234 mm) batteries at Renney and Penlee and Watch House Battery with two 6 inch (152 mm) guns. In the Second World War a number of the new twin 6 pounder anti-motor-torpedo-boat batteries were built, for example the one, again, at Fort Bovisand. The city was also ringed in the war by heavy anti-aircraft batteries such as the one at Down Thomas.

Portland

The important and newly established naval harbour of Portland had been enclosed by a breakwater in 1848, and the first designs for its fortifications were drawn up in 1857 following the threats posed by the new French naval base facing Portland at Cherbourg and the new ironclad *La Gloire*. With Alderney, Rye in Sussex and Dover, it was one of the navy's harbours of refuge. Strong forts were built at the Verne and Nothe, together with a number of lesser works. Two forms of possible attack on Portland had been identified by the Royal Commission, the first one leading to the destruction of its shipping, the second being the seizure of the base following an enemy landing.

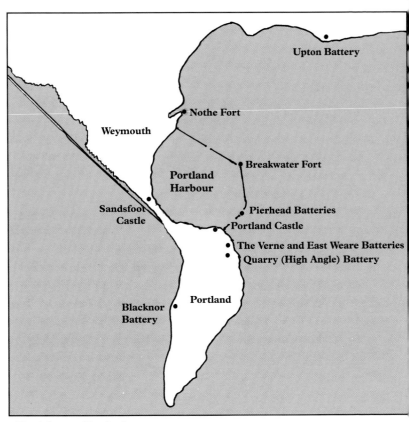

The defences of Portland.

Verne Fort overlooks the Isle and harbour of Portland and is in a naturally strong position above the sea. Some work had started as early as 1848 when the ditch was dug for stone for the breakwater. Building work was carried out partly by convict labour, six hundred convicts working on this and the other defence works at Portland. The cliff's scarp was enhanced, the top of the hill was levelled, and drains and water-supply cisterns were laid. The wartime garrison of one thousand men was accommodated in bombproof, casemated barracks of brick and stone heated by coal grates and provided with a cookhouse, ablutions, a tailor's shop, a sergeants' mess, guardroom and prison. Small married quarters and cottages for the specialist officers (for example the Royal Engineers) completed the accommodation. In addition the fort possessed a hospital, gymnasium, recreation room, museum, lawn tennis courts and cricket ground. The work was also designed to accommodate civilians in an emergency. Its external water supply was vulnerable and was supplemented by internal, rainwater-fed cisterns. The design of the fort was by Captain Crossman, who also produced designs for the fortifications on the Isle of Wight, Portsmouth and Plymouth. At the beginning of the twentieth century the fort was relegated largely to storage, and in the Second World War it was briefly revived as a coastal artillery headquarters. Since 1950 it has been used as a prison.

Entrance into the body of the fort was via a drawbridge, and a further medieval touch was the portcullis worked from a room above the gate. Caponiers protected the ditches and gateway. In 1888 the main permanent armament consisted of rifled muzzle-loading and smooth-bore guns. There was also a 9 inch (229 mm) high-angle rifled muzzle-loader battery outside the fort to supply plunging fire against

Breakwater Fort, Portland, Dorset: part of a rifled muzzle-loading gun can be seen lying at the base of the circular fort, whose gun embrasures are bricked up.

Nothe Fort, Weymouth, Dorset: the entrance to the fort with a musket position above and a caponier to the right, flanking the ditch.

Nothe Fort, Weymouth, Dorset: the interior, showing the rampart and casemated artillery positions. The tall structure on the far left is a Second World War light anti-aircraft position.

the decks of an enemy's armoured warships. In 1906 all of the guns were removed from the fort. The East Weare batteries also formed part of the defences of Verne, situated 200 feet (60 metres) below the fort. The gun crews were accommodated in the fort, from where a solitary path took them to their guns. At the beginning of the twentieth century the battery received two of the new coastal artillery 9.2 inch (234 mm) guns and three 6 inch (152 mm) guns, the former remaining until the standing down of the Royal Artillery coast artillery force in 1956.

For more forward defence Breakwater Fort was completed in 1875. Its construction was not without difficulty, however, as cracks in its masonry foundations had developed following a storm in 1864 and their reinforcement was necessary. A sea fort with iron armoured walls 6.5 feet (2 metres) thick and with internal steam engines for power, it was supplied with 12.5 inch (317 mm) rifled muzzle-loaders, some of which remain nearby, thrown into the sea when they were no longer required. Its later armament consisted of two 6 inch (152 mm) guns and a coastal artillery searchlight on the roof for the examination of shipping.

Nothe Fort was the second major work at Portland, designed to command the channel into Weymouth harbour. Fortifications had been built here in the Civil War. In 1860 the Royal Commission approved the building of a casemated fort, which was to be of a simple 'D' shape of shipped Portland stone. In 1863 the main contractor abruptly left the works and the Royal Engineers took over, aided by convict labour employed in quarrying and shaping the stone. As at the Verne Fort, a drawbridge and portcullis were provided to protect the 4.5 inch (114 mm) timber-and-iron-faced bullet-proof gate. A ditch caponier was also built. In 1872 it was commissioned and armed with four 9 inch (229 mm) and six 10 inch (254 mm) rifled muzzle-loaders. During the Munich Crisis of 1938 it was used as a store for heavy anti-aircraft ammunition, and a 3.7 inch (94 mm) heavy anti-aircraft battery was located outside the fort.

Upton Battery was built in 1902, one of a number of batteries built to protect the harbour. In the Second World War it was rearmed for close defence with two 6 inch (152 mm) ex-naval guns from the Turkish battleship *Reshadieh* (the gun dials remained in Turkish!), which had been taken over in 1914 and renamed HMS *Erin*.

After the end of the First World War the navy was again relied on for national security and the coastal artillery service stagnated: there were fewer guns in position at the start of the Second World War than there had been at the end of the previous war. The arms limitation treaties of the 1920s and 1930s made the reduction in armaments a national policy, and manpower was reduced. Now, in peacetime, all coastal artillery was to be manned by the Territorial Army. In the Second World War two batteries with a pair of 9.2 inch (234 mm) guns were established at Blacknor and East Weare, together with 6 inch (152 mm) batteries at Breakwater Fort, the Nothe and Upton, with a 12 pounder quick-firing battery at the Pierhead. Emergency batteries were emplaced from 1940 onwards along the coast at Brownsea Island, Hengistbury Head, Peveril Point, Abbotsbury and Bridport, with a variety of guns, often ex-naval ones.

Portsmouth

Before the alarms of possible French invasions from the 1840s onwards the seaward defences to the harbour had consisted of Fort Cumberland, protecting Langstone Harbour; Southsea Castle, protecting the harbour approaches; Point Battery, close to the harbour mouth; Fort Monkton and Fort Blockhouse; and the battery at Gilkicker Point. The land defences consisted of the medieval walls of Portsmouth, modernised by de Gomme, and the Portsea and Hilsea Lines, all outdated and in need of repair.

The vital naval harbour and city of Portsmouth is built on an island and until 1940 there was only one road and one railway bridge link with the rest of Hampshire. Portsbridge, crossing the Portscreek, was the key to the island and fortifications were built on either side of the bridgehead. At low tide the protection offered by the creek was diminished. A fort of the Civil War period was rebuilt in 1688 by the Swedish engineer Sir Martin Beckman and in 1746 an earth fort was built on the north bank to protect that side of the bridge. Peter Desmaretz built a fortified line along the north shore of Portsea Island that was completed in 1757, consisting of relatively rudimentary earthworks. In 1845 the London & Brighton Railway Company built

Fort Nelson, Portsmouth: the deep ditch and the roof of a caponier seen from the interior of the fort.

a small redoubt at Hilsea to a Board of Ordnance design in order to protect the position where the railway crossed the line. It consisted of four bastions, two demi-bastions, thirty-six positions for light guns, and a caponier beneath the bridge, but was demolished in 1858. Although protected railway bridges are seen in continental countries, the one at Hilsea was perhaps unique in Britain. In the light of the growing concern with France, Forts Gomer and Elson were built at Gosport in the 1850s, although little thought was given to the updating of the Hilsea defences.

Forts Brockhurst, Grange and Rowner were completed in 1858, forming the Gosport Advanced Line, to protect Portsmouth Harbour and the naval installations on the Gosport Peninsula from an attack from the north-west. Fort Brockhurst, for example, had its offensive armament of nineteen heavy guns on its main ramparts, with eight guns on each flank, four of which were in protected Haxo casemates at rampart level. Nine additional guns in a lower tier crossed fire with the forts at Elson and Rowner. Its circular moated keep provided the main entrance to the work via a drawbridge and was designed as a place of last resort, covering both the interior and the exterior of the fort. The keep was the first of its type to be built in Britain, although the cost of such elaborate structures inhibited their widespread use. Its moat was covered by three caponiers, as well as by the guns in the keep. The fort had two bombproof magazines and accommodation for a garrison of three hundred men. The Gosport forts were incorporated, for financial reasons, into the 1860 Royal Commission proposals, although they were never fully armed, being used mainly for military accommodation and storage.

In 1857 Jervois had drawn up plans for the updating and completion of the defence works at Portsmouth, including the existing Hilsea Lines, which he felt to be 'of weak trace and of low profile'. However, the advent of the breech-loading gun and the French armoured warship *La Gloire* rendered his earlier plans obsolete. The 1860 Royal Commission endorsed the reconstruction of the Lines, this work eventually being completed in 1871, although the armament was not received until 1886. Jervois had given Lieutenant William Crossman the task of designing the new

Fort Nelson, Portsmouth: the Norman-inspired entrance and the finely built walls of brick and knapped flint. A caponier protects the entrance.

Lines; he had previously been involved in the planning of the Great Exhibition of 1851, later designing the Portsdown Hill forts, and becoming Member of Parliament for Portsmouth in 1885. Coffer-dams were built at either end of the creek to deepen it in an emergency. Jervois chose a linear trace with three bastions and two demi-bastions, with outerworks commanded from the principal ramparts: he felt this to be the most appropriate design for the Hilsea Lines despite the obsolescence of this type of fortification. To allow the London road to pass through the Lines two tunnels were built, closed by twin-leafed, iron-studded doors, and a further tunnel allowed the railway to pass through. Although there were guardrooms adjacent to the tunnels, such openings would appear to have compromised the security of the Lines. The armament consisted of 168 32 pounder casemated smooth-bores plus a number of rifled and muzzle-loading guns, some on Moncrieff disappearing carriages. The latter used an ingenious mirror-sighting mechanism that allowed the gun layer to observe the target while he was out of sight. The heavy guns had been withdrawn by 1903, such linear defences being thoroughly out of favour by the time the original armament had been delivered. In the First World War the Lines were armed with four Maxim .303 machine-guns to guard the road and rail links against enemy raiding parties. After the fall of France in 1940 all crossing points were mined, and if an invasion had occurred the Lines would have acted as Portsmouth's outer landward line of defence.

The advent of the rifled and long-range Armstrong breech-loading gun meant that none of the existing fortifications – neither the old Hilsea Lines nor the newly proposed line of forts between Gomer and Elson on the Gosport peninsula – would be sufficiently forward to protect the dockyards from bombardment. A committee had met in February 1859 to consider the probable influences of the new rifled gun on Portsmouth's defences. It recommended an arc of forts from Chichester Harbour to Fareham Creek, plus two on the Gosport peninsula; the Needles Passage was also considered for refortification. The Royal Commission, making its report in 1860, took over from this committee and considered the defence of the nation's harbours

Fort Nelson, Portsmouth: a parapet-mounted smooth-bore, muzzle-loading gun on a traversing carriage with Haxo casemates beyond.

and dockyards in general. It stated several concerns about Portsmouth and proposed the following five actions: first, the immediate protection of the harbour entrance; second, the prevention of an enemy gaining a footing between Browndown and Fort Cumberland; third, the protection of the Spithead anchorage and the dockyard against bombardment from Spithead; fourth, the defence of the Needles Passage; fifth, the prevention of landings on the Isle of Wight. There was felt to be an especial need for the building of sea forts, as well as a need to defend Portsdown Hill, although the earlier works of the 1850s in the Gosport region were considered to be worth retaining. Portsmouth accounted for the major part of the Commission's proposed expenditure: £2 million out of a total budget of £9 million. A wartime garrison of fifteen thousand men would be required for Portsmouth, with five thousand for the Isle of Wight.

The massive proposed expenditure did not please the Chancellor of the Exchequer, Gladstone, who threatened to resign. However, Palmerston, the Prime Minister, stood his ground, telling a sympathetic Queen Victoria that he 'would rather lose Gladstone than the Portsmouth fortifications'. Although Gladstone relented, there still remained strong parliamentary opposition to the Commission's proposals. Opponents termed the fortifications 'Palmerston's Follies'. The 'Blue Water School', as we have seen, did not believe that the French could ever land, given the power of the navy. Captain Cowper Coles MP claimed that the proposed sea forts, with their short-range guns, would be inadequate even if they were able to see their prey beyond the smoke produced by their own guns. Recent naval actions in the American Civil War between the armoured gunboats *Merrimac* and *Monitor* had shown the growing strength of this new generation of fighting ship.

The Defence Commission stuck by its contentions but work was largely suspended on the Commission fortifications during the debates. Despite the ongoing disagreements some work had begun at Portsdown, and final governmental agreement on all of the points was reached in 1863. However, there were still practical problems and delays – for example at Fort Purbrook and at Fort Wallington, where the foundations had subsided. In the spring of 1864 work began on sea forts to protect Spithead, four eventually being built after severe practical problems: Spitbank Fort, Nomansland Fort, Horse Sand Fort, and the smaller St Helen's Fort, which was located off the Isle of Wight. All of the forts were complete by 1880. By 1867 the work at Portsmouth was well under way, although delays would arise engendered by the recent advances in artillery design. The Portsdown forts of Purbrook, Widley,

Spitbank Fort, the Solent: one of the Palmerston sea forts protecting approaches to Portsmouth Harbour.

Hurst Castle, Hampshire: a detail of one of the granite artillery casemates, the rust stain marking the position of the teak and iron shield.

Southwick, Nelson and Wallington, as well as the detached Fort Fareham, with their deep ditches, low profiles, Haxo casemates, traverses, and gate and ditch protection, were at the time among the most modern and impressive fortifications in the world. The spirit of the Victorian age is reflected in their mightiness, and also in more revealing, minor details: for example, the influence of the Gothic revival is shown by the Romanesque gateway and arched mural arcading at Fort Nelson.

The Isle of Wight and the Needles defences

The Needles Passage guarded the 'back door' to Southampton and Portsmouth. It possessed natural strength in that it presented a narrow shipping channel where the Shingles Shoal and the underwater Needles Rocks met. Powerful tides were also found here but these could equally take enemy ships through the channel. On the other hand, the unstable nature of the geology of the Isle of Wight presented both difficulties – in the building of its defences – and also advantages – in that the steep cliffs made enemy landings difficult.

Throughout the seventeenth and eighteenth centuries the Henrician castles at Hurst in Hampshire and Yarmouth on the island represented the sole defence of the Needles Passage: while the latter would not see further development, Hurst would give service up to the middle of the twentieth century. Hurst was at the eastern end of a long pebble spit where the shipping channel narrows and was briefly one of the prisons of Charles I. In the late eighteenth century earth-protected batteries were added. In 1806 the keep of the castle was vaulted to support six 24 pounder guns, and in the 1850s caponiers, new casemates and shell-firing smooth-bore guns were provided.

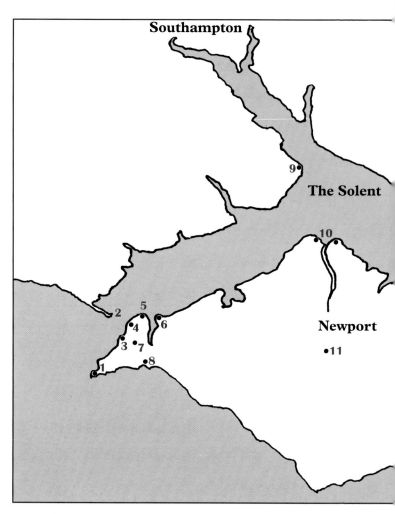

In the 1850s further work took place on the island with the construction between 1852 and 1855 of Fort Victoria, a redan-shaped brick battery built to cover the deep-water channel. Horseshoe-shaped, with a casemated battery, it resembled some of the forts seen at Sebastopol during the Crimean War. A glacis sloped from the fort's ditch to seaward. Between 1854 and 1856 Fort Albert (also known as Cliff End Fort) was built, a small multi-tiered brick fort situated at the water's edge. Freshwater Redoubt, also known as Golden Hill Fort, was built as a defensible barracks in 1855–6 to cover the rear areas of the two forts, as well as to cover the only reasonable landing-place behind the Needles defences. It also accommodated the adjacent batteries' garrisons in peacetime. However, these three relatively weak works were quickly to be rendered obsolete by the introduction of the ironclad warship and the new generation of rifled guns.

In 1860 the Royal Commission made its recommendations with regard to the Needles defences: two new batteries would be built and earlier works refurbished. Hurst Castle was massively rebuilt as a curved casemated battery, the casemates giving protection to its guns from naval enfilade fire: the Commission had, among other points, condemned open batteries as being too vulnerable to such attack. The massive single-storey granite casemated block was designed to take sixty-one guns,

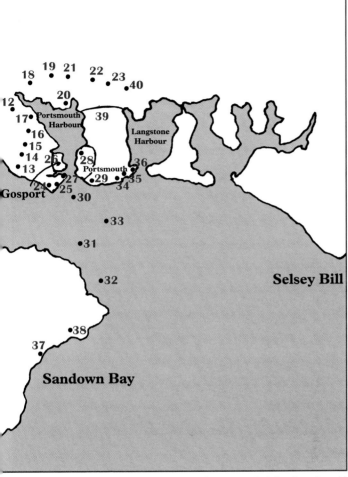

The defences of the Isle of Wight, Solent and Portsmouth (after Saunders, 1989).

1.	Needles Old and New Batteries	21.	Fort Southwick
2.	Hurst Castle	22.	Fort Widley
3.	Warden Point Battery	23.	Fort Purbrook
4.	Fort Albert/Cliff End Battery	24.	Gilkicker Fort
5.	Fort Victoria	25.	Fort Monckton
6.	Yarmouth Castle	26.	Gosport Lines
7.	Golden Hill Fort	27.	Fort Blockhouse
8.	Freshwater Bay Redoubt	28.	Portsea/Portsmouth Lines
9.	Calshot Castle	29.	Southsea Castle
10.	West and East Cowes Castles	30.	Spitbank Fort
11.	Carisbrooke Castle	31.	Nomansland Fort
12.	Fort Fareham	32.	St Helen's Fort
13.	Fort Gomer	33.	Horse Sand Fort
14.	Fort Grange	34.	Lumps Fort Battery
15.	Fort Rowner	35.	Eastney Batteries
16.	Fort Brockhurst	36.	Fort Cumberland
17.	Fort Elson	37.	Sandown Fort
18.	Fort Wallington	38.	Bembridge Fort
19.	Fort Nelson	39.	Hilsea Lines
20.	Portchester Castle	40.	Farlington Redoubt

Fort Albert, Isle of Wight: a fort of the 1850s, considered to be thoroughly outmoded by the 1860 Royal Commission report. The fort was part of the Needles defences, facing Hurst Castle.

later to be protected behind iron shields, the battery's rear being protected by a massive wall. The Henrician castle was retained as an infantry keep and magazine. Progress was, however, slow: it was only in 1874 that a reduced number of guns and their shields arrived at Hurst Castle. In 1885 the castle's armament consisted of twelve 12.5 inch (317 mm), twenty-three 10 inch (254 mm) and five 9 inch (229 mm) rifled muzzle-loaders, plus seven 64 pounder gorge guns. In the Second World War both Hurst Castle and Fort Albert mounted twin 6 pounder quick-firing batteries to protect the Solent from enemy torpedo boats. In 1876 Fort Victoria was disarmed and

Old Needles Battery, Isle of Wight: in the immediate foreground is a position-finder cell, the 9 inch and 7 inch rifled muzzle-loader positions are below right, and the tall building at the top of the photograph was the port war signal station.

converted into a submarine mining depot. Fort Albert was converted into a Brennan torpedo station twelve years later, this unusual wire-propelled and guided weapon enjoying only a brief service life at this and a small number of other sites.

The Needles Point Battery was built between 1861 and 1863 and covered the Needles Passage and the Alum Bay beach. Because of the fragile nature of the bedrock no gun larger than the 9 inch (229 mm) rifled muzzle-loader could be installed, this armament being unceremoniously dumped into the sea when the New Needles Battery was built at the end of the nineteenth century. A number of the guns were subsequently recovered in the 1960s and restored and are now displayed at Southsea Castle, Fort Widley and Fort Brockhurst. The battery's magazines were placed under an artificial chalk mound, which also acted as the terreplein and traverse for the guns and barracks. In 1913 the first British experimental anti-aircraft gun was trialled here. The New Needles Battery was built a short distance from the earlier battery between 1893 and 1895 and was armed with two 9.2 inch (234 mm) guns to command the sea approaches to the Solent, and in 1941 overhead cover was added to the guns.

Following the recommendations of the 1905 Owen Committee, the different types of coastal artillery had been given dedicated tasks in order to keep enemy warships at maximum ranges: for example, the Warden Point and New Needles Batteries had heavy 9.2 inch (234 mm) guns for counter bombardment fire against battleships, while other batteries had 6 inch (152 mm) guns for use against enemy cruisers and destroyers. Hurst Castle had 6 pounder quick-firing guns for use against light and fast torpedo boats. The 9.2 inch, 6 inch and twin 6 pounder would remain the principal armament of the many coastal batteries built to protect the ports, docks and naval harbours of Britain and her Empire in the twentieth century until the standing down of the coastal artillery force in 1956.

Elsewhere on the island the 1860 Royal Commission had identified the Sandown area, as had Henry VII's advisers, as an ideal invasion landing area, and in 1861 the construction began of Sandown Granite Fort. Its guns were in casemates, with the iron shields arriving later. The dry ditch was covered by caponiers. In the Second World War it sheltered the PLUTO (Pipeline Under The Ocean) terminal. Also in the Sandown area, in the nineteenth century, batteries were sited at Yaverland, Sandown Barracks and Redcliff. In the 1860s Bembridge Fort was the only substantial Victorian land work on the island. It was hexagonal in plan, with a brick-lined ditch and caponiers, and was armed with 64 pounder rifled muzzle-loaders. In the Second World War the fort was used to control underwater indicator loops and to house Asdic equipment to warn of submarine or motor torpedo boat incursions on the Spithead area. Some close defence protection was provided at the fort in the war – Spigot mortars and an Allan Williams steel machine-gun turret. In the twentieth century Culver Cliff battery was established with two 9.2 inch (234 mm) guns, with magazines below and protected by a Twydall Profile. In the Second World War it housed a port war signal station and a combined battery command post. Contemporary with this site was Yaverland Battery, also armed with two 9.2 inch guns. From 1942 it saw the introduction of coast defence radar for the sighting of targets at night and in all weather conditions.

Dover

Dover, facing the Catholic continent, had a number of Henrician fortifications, namely Moats Bulwark, Archcliffe Fort and the Black Bulwark. To an enemy not equipped with artillery the ancient castle still represented a formidable obstacle. Even in the Second World War the castle and its developed defences presented and were turned into a significant anti-tank barrier.

The need to protect the vulnerable Western Heights had been seen at the time of the outbreak of war with France in 1793, a period in which vast amounts of money were also being spent on updating the castle's defences. Lieutenant Colonel Twiss

Dover, Western Heights: the Drop Redoubt, an early-nineteenth-century casemated barracks with caponiers (foreground) added in the 1850s. The mighty bulk of Dover Castle is in the background, to the left.

added additional defences in the form of the Horseshoe and Hudson's Bastion and the East Demi-Bastion, as well as elaborate underground defences connecting with the Spur. The resumption of war with France in 1803 and the real prospect of invasion led to the construction of fieldworks on the Heights as well as three powerful works, the Citadel, the North Central Bastion and the pentagonal Drop Redoubt. By the time of the 1860 Royal Commission the defences were still incomplete. The Commission called for their completion, together with all outworks, the completion of the lines between the Drop Redoubt and the Citadel, the remodelling of parts of the Heights to improve visibility and to reduce dead ground, and the construction of Fort Burgoyne, the South Lines and the South Entrance. The works were complete by 1873. In 1886 the Drop Redoubt possessed eleven 7 inch (178 mm) rifled breech-loaders.

The Citadel is a large, irregular-shaped work with bombproof officers' quarters and an internal keep as a place of last refuge, although its position on the edge of

The Dover Turret on Admiralty Pier: this view shows the layered, armoured construction of the turret via the open cover of one of the two gun positions.

the cliff made it very vulnerable to the new generation of rifled cannon appearing in the middle of the century. Fort Burgoyne was built to protect the north front of the Western Heights; of a 'V' shape, it showed an early use of concrete in the revetment of its ditches. The Western Outwork was built to protect the western side of the Citadel; these two works, as well as the earlier Drop Redoubt, were provided with caponiers. Towards the end of the century reliance for the defence of Dover started to switch to coastal batteries, new ones being located at the Western Heights, St Martins, Archcliffe, Langdon Cliff, South Front and South Lines. Before the start of the Second World War more modern batteries were built at Dover: South Front Battery, with three 6 inch (152 mm) guns, and Citadel Battery, with three 9.2 inch (234 mm) guns.

However, the most remarkable work built at the port was the unique Dover Turret. In 1867 Jervois had ordered the building of a 'small fort' at the end of the new Admiralty Pier at Dover. In 1870 it was proposed, instead, that a turret mounting two of the most powerful guns available be built on the pier. In 1872 diving bells prepared the foundations on the harbour bed. The weapon chosen for the turret was a gun designed originally for HMS *Inflexible*, the 16 inch (406 mm) rifled muzzle-loader of 80 tons. Remarkably, full information on the performance of this new and devastating weapon had appeared in civil engineering periodicals at the time of its unveiling in 1876. Produced at the Royal Gun Factory in Woolwich, the outer barrel consisted of hammered and welded coils; the barrel was machined from a 16.5 ton block of Sheffield steel, rifled, and with the breech and trunnions shrunk on. This very expensive gun required twice its own weight of metal for its production. The guns were moved on special artillery barges to Shoeburyness for trials. By 1881 the turret, built by the Thames Ironworks, was substantially complete. A number of steam engines powered the turret: one moved ammunition to the muzzles, one ran the guns back after recoil and dealt with the elevation and depression of the guns, while another rotated the turret. There were also an auxiliary engine and a donkey engine to work the pumps. In May 1882 the final gun was installed. These guns are the only surviving examples of the 80 ton gun, although the steam engines were removed long ago. Such very large guns required prodigious quantities of gunpowder, and from the late 1880s the more powerful and efficient propellant cordite began to replace gunpowder.

Coalhouse Fort, Essex: the entrance to the fort protected by the defensible barrack block.

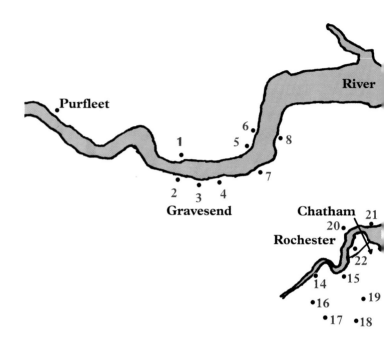

The Thames defences

Before the advent of the railways and in an age of poor roads the River Thames had been the gateway to the capital, a vital commercial artery as well as containing, on its edge, the Woolwich Arsenal, the Deptford revictualling yard and the Purfleet powder magazine. To guard the approaches to his capital, Henry VIII had built five small bulwarks at West and East Tilbury; in the following century there were also the important forts at Tilbury and New Tavern. In 1868 the remodelling of the old Tilbury and New Tavern forts began as recommended by the Royal Commission, and by 1874 the armament of both forts consisted of 12 inch (305 mm) and 9 inch (229 mm) rifled muzzle-loaders. From the late eighteenth century the outer defences of the Thames had begun to be pushed out to the forts at Shornemead, Cliffe and Coalhouse.

The Royal Commission's report recommended that the old fort at Coalhouse be demolished and replaced by a new work, with additional works at Shornemead and Cliffe Creek to form a triangle of fire, together with a boom defence and a minefield. Coalhouse Fort was provided with the now common curved, massive and armoured casemates with 5 feet (1.5 metres) thick roofs as a protection against plunging fire, a defensible barracks at the gorge and an open battery up-river. A water-filled outer ditch and inner dry ditch were protected by caponiers. Trees were planted around the fort in the 1870s to act as a form of camouflage. Colonel Gordon, later to become famous as General Gordon of Khartoum, supervised the final stages of the works at Coalhouse from New Tavern Fort, which was armed with ten 9 inch (229 mm) rifled muzzle-loaders, crossing its fire with Tilbury Fort. Coalhouse Fort's armament in the 1870s consisted of twenty rifled muzzle-loaders, capable of penetrating the sides of an armoured warship. The guns had ranges of up to 3.4 miles (5.5 km) and were mounted on metal carriages with gears for elevation and traversing. Pistons slowed the recoil of the guns. In the 1880s a battery command post was added to the roof

The defences of the Thames and Medway (after Saunders, 1989).

1. Tilbury Fort
2. Gravesend Blockhouse
3. New Tavern Fort
4. Milton Blockhouse
5. Coalhouse Fort/East Tilbury Battery
6. Higham Blockhouse
7. Shornemead Fort
8. Cliffe Fort
9. Slough Fort
10. Grain Fort
11. Grain Tower
12. Garrison Point Fort/Sheerness Lines
13. Shoeburyness Battery
14. Fort Clarence
15. Fort Pitt
16. Fort Borstal
17. Fort Bridgewoods
18. Fort Horstead
19. Fort Luton
20. Upnor Castle
21. Cockham Wood Fort
22. Fort Amherst/Chatham Lines
23. Gillingham Fort
24. Fort Darland
25. Twydall Redoubts
26. Hoo Fort
27. Darnet Fort

of the fort, orders being given to the casemates via voice-tubes. In 1897 the fort's battery command post received one of the new depression rangefinders. The height above sea level on any given date could be determined by referring to Admiralty tidal charts, and the angle of depression of the instrument to the target then gave its range by means of triangulation. The later depression position finder, introduced at the beginning of the following century, enabled the speed and bearing of the target also to be computed. At about the same time as the introduction of the depression rangefinder Coalhouse Fort received four of the new 6 inch (152 mm) coastal guns, which had a range of 7 miles (11 km), plus four 12 pounder quick-firing guns. The fort also benefited from the introduction at the end of the nineteenth century of the coast artillery searchlight, powered by generators. The introduction of searchlights, minefields and more up-to-date guns gave the fort, and others of the time, a formidable defensive and offensive capability.

Magazines were lit from glazed lamp recesses accessed via external lighting passages. Lamps that contained a candle, kept in position by being forced up by a spring, were inserted into the recesses from the passages. Non-ferrous metals were used to avoid sparks and wood was used to line magazine walls and floors, the crews changing into special magazine clothing. A detached building called a laboratory made up the cartridges used to ignite the propellant charges in the guns. In an emergency the crews lived by their guns, as in the time of Henry VIII. By the 1880s European warships had become more heavily armoured and armed, and the closely packed guns and vertical faces of the casemated batteries were now becoming vulnerable.

The new East Tilbury Battery of 1891 indicated the new way of thinking on the protection of coastal batteries. Situated on gently sloping ground, almost hidden from view, and with a Twydall Profile developed by the Royal Engineers for the new infantry positions at Chatham, the battery was surrounded by a shallow ditch within which was an unclimbable fence. The armament consisted of two 10 inch (254 mm) and four 6 inch (152 mm) breech-loaders. Harder hitting, with a higher rate of fire and a longer range (8750 yards; 8000 metres), the guns were hidden in deep pits and on disappearing carriages. The latter were now raised by compressed air, an improvement on the earlier Moncrieff system that had used counterweights. In 1889 the introduction of smokeless-powder propellant charges further aided the camouflaging of the batteries. In 1903 the battery received the new 6 inch (152 mm) coastal artillery gun, which was now on a simple, non-disappearing pedestal mounting, firing *en barbette*.

Chatham

The ring of forts proposed by the Royal Commission for Chatham has the distinction of being the location where the last large fort was built in Britain. In their simplified, flattened-arrowhead form they resembled fortifications of the period built in Germany, France and Austro-Hungary, all soon to be made obsolete by the German *feste* system at the end of the nineteenth century. As at the other Commission forts, firepower was to be directed towards the frontal and flanking fields. Work on the Chatham defences proceeded slowly and in the 1880s stopped entirely, recommencing in 1887. The 1860 Royal Commission report on Chatham had proposed for the eastern defences forts at Star Hill (Fort Darland), Gillingham (Twydall Redoubts), Luton (Fort Luton), Bridgwood (Fort Horstead) and Cookham (Fort Bridgewoods), all to be approximately a mile and a half apart and provided with all-round defence. For the western defences a line of forts was planned between the Medway and the Thames, although only one fort was built. Two sea forts were also built, at Hoo and Darnet, although these sites were not the original nominated locations, marshy conditions forcing the abandonment of the earlier plans. The Commission calculated a requirement for a wartime establishment of 417 guns and 4650 men, at a total cost of £1.6 million. A light railway was built to assist in the building of the entire line.

In 1869 a parliamentary committee reported on the progress of the works, many of the fortifications planned for the Medway and Thames line having been cancelled by then. The number of guns allocated to each work was reduced from twenty-five to eleven after the substitution of the heavier rifled muzzle-loaders for the smooth-bores. Construction was often difficult because of the marshy nature of the ground, which led to subsidence and dampness within the works. The eastern defences were deferred to the 1870s because of budgetary constraints. As with the other Commission fortifications, the principal works were polygonal in trace, with straight sides, dry ditches, caponiers and counterscarp galleries, but simpler in design and earth-covered for better camouflage. Work on the Chatham defences was complete by 1900, but by 1910 their decline had already started.

Of all of the forts, that at Borstal was considered to be the best sited. The new fort was agreed after the cancellation of the proposed works between the earlier Forts Pitt and Clarence. The building work was done mainly by convict labour, and from 1875 the fort was used as a prison, later named the 'Borstal Institution'. In 1939 the ramparts carried a battery of the new 4.5 inch (114 mm) heavy anti-aircraft guns for the defence of the Chatham dockyard. At Fort Bridgewoods work started in 1879 but was halted in 1884, when almost complete, because of a lack of money and official enthusiasm: the work was finally finished in 1892. In the Royal Engineers' siege operations of 1907 the fort came off badly, the main counterscarp gallery being blown in by the 'attackers'. The purpose of the operations was to gain practical knowledge of siege techniques, including mining and countermining; the use of searchlights; and the blowing-in of counterscarp galleries, together with practice infantry assaults on the forts. The 'Red Army' provided the defence force while the 'Blue Army' were the attackers. The conclusion was reached that the fortifications were not invincible but would slow down an invader sufficiently to enable the defenders to regroup and counter-attack. In October 1939, while in use as a military wireless intercept station, Fort Bridgewoods was hit by enemy bombs. In 1953 it was the site of the underground Regional Seat of Government for south London, but it was considered to be too close to Chatham, a likely nuclear target, and was closed down on the reorganisation of the UK Warning and Monitoring Organisation.

Fort Horsted, the largest of the forts, defended the main London road but was never permanently armed. The fort's mobile armament in time of war consisted of eight 8 inch (203 mm) and four 6.6 inch (168 mm) howitzers, twelve 20 pounder rifled breech-loaders, thirteen 64 pounder rifled muzzle-loaders and twelve 32 pounder smooth-bores for the counterscarp galleries. No caponiers were fitted as by the time of its construction these were increasingly felt to be vulnerable to howitzer fire. Fort Luton overlooked the valley that gave the fort its name, the main approach route to Chatham. A rolling bridge on wheels, crossing the ditch, could be winched back into the fort and then turned through 90 degrees to close the gateway. The size of the fort was reduced during its building, and the ditches were lined in concrete. The fort was also used in the 1907 practice siege operations, a section of the ditch being mined, and the resulting breach was 'stormed'. In the Second World War the fort accommodated an Anti-Aircraft Command headquarters. Fort Darland was the last to be built at Chatham, and in Britain, completed in 1899 with the most modern armament of the Chatham defences. This was now more mobile in nature, with quick-firing guns and machine-guns for close defence. The bridge giving entry to the fort ran on top of the solitary caponier. Unlike the other forts, this was built by civilian contractors rather than by convict labour. In the Second World War the fort was used as a massive air-raid shelter by the local civilian population. The forts of Hoo and Darnet were built on two islands in the Medway. Of circular plan, they contained two tiers of 9 inch (229 mm) rifled muzzle-loading guns for all-round fire. They proved difficult building sites, the ground beneath them shifting, and each work required reinforcement by the placing of thick iron bands around its walls.

In addition to the forts, between 1886 and 1889 two semi-permanent infantry redoubts had been built by the Royal Engineers at Twydall. The concept of such redoubts had arisen in the 1870s during the Russo-Turkish War, when concentrated rifle fire from infantry protected by hastily dug earthworks had proved sufficient to throw back the Russian attackers. The attractive feature of these unobtrusive works was that they could be built rapidly in times of danger to provide concentrated infantry fire for nearby mobile artillery batteries. Their ditches possessed an almost vertical face to the field, at the base of which was a continuous, unclimbable fence. Infantry shelters, open at their rears, were made shellproof by a reinforced concrete roof, the whole covered by an earth mound. The Twydall Profile would be used at other locations, such as in the design of the London Mobilisation Centres. The use of civilian contract labour was specified, each work was to be ready within one month of the contract being given, and construction was to be by hand tools only. Military opinion at the time did, however, consider that such works were too weak, and that the infantry would be too exposed to hostile fire.

Within a few years of the completion of the Chatham Line, the smashing of the modern forts at Liège in Belgium in 1914 by the German army demonstrated that an enemy with powerful siege guns could reduce relatively new forts to rubble. In any event, the usefulness of the Chatham forts was questionable: the Government had refused to arm them adequately, even though their artillery cost much less than the works themselves, and there was an overall lack of uniformity in their design, most being too small to resist a prolonged attack. By the First World War they were of little significance as the anti-invasion defence of the area had shifted to the Maidstone–Sittingbourne Line, defended by fieldworks for infantry and artillery.

Harwich

For hundreds of years the Orwell Haven had been the only safe anchorage between the Thames and the Humber. Harwich retained its medieval walls, and two blockhouses, part of Henry VIII's coastal defences, had been built in the 1540s. A period of neglect followed before the first Landguard Fort was built in 1625, together with the Half Moon Battery, both covering the harbour. Repairs to the

Landguard Fort, Suffolk: the curved casemates and unusual bull-nosed caponier of the 1870s Royal Commission remodelling. One of the bastions of the 1740 work is shown projecting into the ditch, above the caponier.

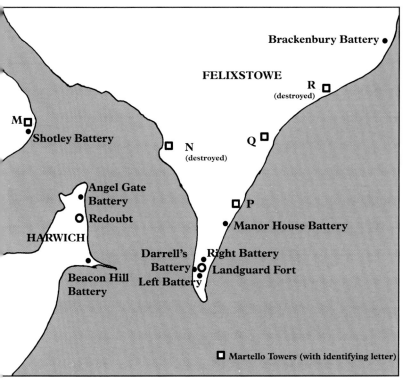

The defences of Harwich.

town's defences were carried out after the Second Dutch War. Landguard had been given a new earthen bastioned trace to a design by de Gomme, and in 1667 it was unsuccessfully attacked by the Dutch. A further period of neglect took place, the defence of the town resting entirely on Landguard Fort. In 1717 the fort was rebuilt, in a closed lunette shape with a ten-gun battery. Following the Jacobean uprising in 1745 it was rebuilt again with a bastioned pentagonal trace and a small barrack block and governor's house, and later two flanking batteries were added. In the mid nineteenth century General Burgoyne had felt that Landguard was an 'old and very defective work, with barracks vulnerable to cannon fire'. The rebuilt Landguard Fort had been criticised for having bastions that were too small, and casemates and ramparts too weak to support artillery. This latter failing had been partially corrected by the building of the adjacent Beauclerk's Battery. In 1807 the fort's ramparts were rebuilt to take 32 pounders. During the period of the Royal Commission, between 1871 and 1872, radical changes took place: a semicircular defensible barrack block was built and, more dramatically, a casemated front of granite was constructed to accommodate rifled muzzle-loaders. Below the casemates, in the ditch, was built an unusual, bull-nosed caponier. In 1888 and 1889 the artillery defences of Landguard were further strengthened by the building of the Right and Left Batteries. In the late nineteenth century a part of the fort was converted for the operation of a manually controlled minefield. Darrell's Battery was built in front of the fort in 1901, ending the fort's role as an effective fortification. In 1940 twin 6 pounders and a director tower were sited at Darrell's Battery. In the twentieth century it became the fire control headquarters of the Harwich defences, as well as a port war signal station.

Landguard Fort, Suffolk: the 1875 entrance to the new barracks and casemated front. A drawbridge would have crossed the small semicircular ditch.

During the period of the Royal Commission, Harwich Redoubt was rearmed with 68 pounders and 8 inch (203 mm) smooth-bores, and there was a new battery at Shotley and the Martello and adjacent batteries were also rearmed. In 1861 the level of defence for the Orwell Haven had been judged to be totally inadequate. Colonel Jervois proposed a fourteen-gun battery with earth ramparts, a ditch and loopholed Carnot wall at Shotley. The battery was not designed for permanent manning but would be manned by the Norfolk Volunteers in wartime. In 1890 it was armed with four 10 inch (254 mm) rifled muzzle-loaders but by 1911 these guns had gone. The Owen Committee in 1905 had recommended the reclassification of Harwich as a commercial port, but this was reconsidered with the growing concern of the navy for the safety of its new fuel depots and destroyer and light cruiser anchorages. Brackenbury Battery was rearmed with a heavier armament of two 9.2 inch (234 mm) guns. In radar trials in 1939 at Bawdsey the fall of shot from the battery could be seen on the radar set: it would now be possible for coastal artillery to obtain a target's range and bearing, and later trials witnessed the shell in flight on a radar screen.

In the latter part of the nineteenth century the threat from France began to be eclipsed following the creation of the new German Empire under Bismarck. Harwich, facing the North Sea, had also become the fourth most important port in Britain. Although Landguard Fort had for centuries been the key to Harwich there was a need for an opposing battery to close the gap on the other side of the Orwell. In 1888 work began at Beacon Hill. By this time modern warships could pulverise forts such as the recently modernised Landguard. It was becoming apparent that a cheaper, less substantial design for batteries would be more efficient. Beacon Hill was somewhat isolated from the main Harwich garrison and would therefore require its own land defences. The building of the battery was a test of new ideas: its breech-loading guns were on modern hydro-pneumatic disappearing carriages, which appeared above the parapet only for twenty seconds in order to fire. The guns were enclosed in concrete aproned gun pits, with a layer of sand in front of the apron to absorb enemy shot. Quick-firing guns were emplaced too, to deal with enemy small craft and to stop landing parties of enemy marines, and to support the infantry defence on land. Leaving the site largely in its natural state provided a degree of camouflage and an artificial hill gave protection to the guns from the rear, this also providing cover for the engine room and shelters, with fire steps for the infantry. A Twydall

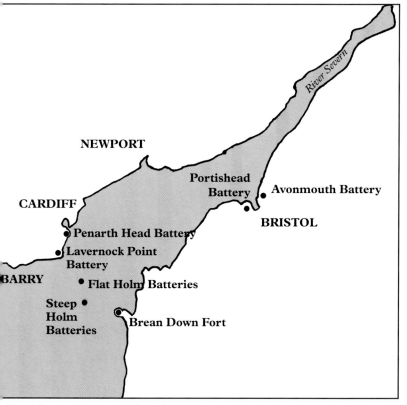

The defences of the Bristol Channel.

Profile protected the site, with an 8 foot (2.4 metre) high steel fence hidden in the scarped ditch that was built in the glacis. The Owen Committee had swept away the proliferation of old guns in the nation's fortifications, and at Beacon Hill the new pedestal-mounted, low-profile 6 inch (152 mm) coast artillery gun replaced the earlier guns on their disappearing carriages. The usual suite of fire-control positions and searchlights was installed. In addition, a twin 6 pounder position with director tower was added in 1940, named Cornwallis Battery.

The Bristol Channel defences

The defences built in the Bristol Channel protected the western ports of Bristol, Barry, Cardiff and Swansea. These faced away from continental Europe and therefore did not receive the same level of protection as Britain's southern and eastern ports, so avoiding the expensive land defences seen elsewhere. We have seen that the French Revolutionary and Napoleonic Wars between 1793 and 1815 were a period of great peril for Britain and in 1797 there was a French incursion to sack Bristol and other west-coast ports, a party landing in Pembrokeshire but quickly surrendering. In the same year a gun battery was built at Avonmouth to protect the river mouth and crossed fire with another battery at Portishead.

The 1860 Royal Commission report proposed a number of new batteries on the islands of Steep Holm and Flat Holm, which would connect their fire with the new mainland batteries at Brean Down and Lavernock Point, the latter having 7 inch (178 mm) rifled muzzle-loaders on Moncrieff disappearing carriages. This ordnance, introduced with the other calibres of muzzle-loaders to replace the unsuccessful Armstrong breech-loading gun, could adequately cover the Severn Estuary. Other, more minor, batteries, including Second World War emergency batteries, would be sited to protect specific docks and ports such as those at Barry and Swansea.

Brean Down Fort in Somerset was built in 1867 at the tip of a promontory and was provided with a 12 foot (3.7 metre) deep ditch spanned by a rolling bridge. Its armament consisted of seven 7 inch (178 mm) rifled muzzle-loaders in three separate positions. There were two accommodation blocks facing the ditch and holding fifty-one men and twenty horses. The normally uneventful life of a fort's garrison was shattered at Brean Down in July 1900 when the 'Brean Down Disaster' occurred. Gunner Haines, a man of a reportedly violent disposition, apparently took his own life by discharging a rifle into the number three powder magazine, the resultant explosion not only killing him but also badly damaging part of the fort. This event effectively ended the life of the fort, its guns being removed the following year. In the Second World War the fort accommodated a battery of two 6 inch (152 mm) coastal artillery guns.

At Steep Holm work began in 1866 to fortify the island. Barracks for fifty men were built, an underground cistern providing water for the soldiers. Four batteries were built on the island, initially, as at Flat Holm, for the 7 inch (178 mm) rifled muzzle-loaders, but later these were replaced by the new Armstrong 6 inch (152 mm) coastal artillery gun. In the same year work began on the island of Flat Holm, this also receiving four batteries, nine of the guns being on Moncrieff carriages. In 1903 the island also received the new Armstrong 6 inch coastal artillery breech-loading guns. Perhaps the most momentous event involving the Severn defences was of a non-military nature, when in May 1897 Marconi sent a message by the revolutionary new means of wireless telegraphy from Flat Holm to Lavernock Point. In the Second World War the islands supported coastal and anti-aircraft guns intended to stop enemy aircraft and naval craft from attacking the shipping and important ports of the Bristol Channel.

Milford Haven

Apart from the two blockhouses built in 1580 by Henry VIII, this area had seen little further development until the nineteenth century. In 1813 the Admiralty decided to establish a major dockyard in Milford Haven and in 1817 a study by Major General Bryce recommended the establishment of batteries and the building of three towers,

Stack Rock Fort, Milford Haven: one of two sea forts protecting the Haven. The fort, incorporating a smaller work of the 1850s, was originally designed for a double bank of artillery casemates but only one gun deck was built, the other level being used for barrack space.

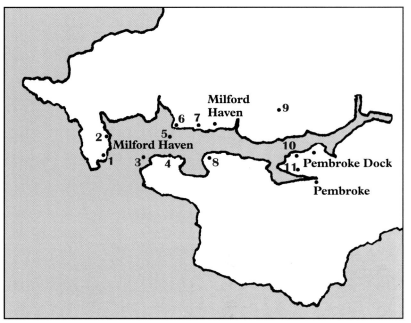

The defences of Milford Haven.

1.	West Blockhouse Fort	7. Hubberston Fort
2.	Dale Fort	8. Popton Fort
3.	Thorn Island Fort	9. Fort Scoveston
4.	Chapel Bay Battery	10. Pembroke Dock Towers
5.	Stack Rock Fort	11. Defensible Barracks
6.	South Hook Fort	

but nothing was done. There was also an early appreciation of the need to protect the landward approaches to Pembroke Dock. In 1841 construction began on a bastioned defensible barracks to hold the Royal Marines, who guarded the dockyard, above Pembroke Dock, its walls and ramparts pierced by many musket loopholes. In the First World War it served as a siege-warfare training school.

With the further development of the dockyard, as well as tension with the United States, came the need for additional defences. Two towers were built between 1848 and 1850 in the waters of the dockyard, named the North East Gun Tower and the South West Gun Tower. A tower for three guns was also built on Stack Rock. The towers were of differing designs: one was polygonal (the south-western one), while the other two were roughly oval in shape. They were built of brick with limestone and granite masonry facings and mounted three 32 pounder guns on their roofs plus 12 pounders internally to protect the dock wall flanks. Because of mistakes in designing the roof gun mountings, the guns were not installed until 1855. The North East Tower had a shot furnace and in the Second World War was used to mount light anti-aircraft guns, engaging German aircraft attacking the Haven. Between 1850 and 1857 work also began on the fortifications at Thorn Island, Dale Fort and West Blockhouse Fort, all of them becoming quickly obsolete with the introduction of rifled cannon.

In December 1858 a report was presented to Parliament on the harbour defences of Milford Haven and Pembroke Dock, drawn up by a committee appointed by the Secretary of State for War. In addition to the works mentioned above, two new lines

Thorn Island Fort, Milford Haven: part of the mid-nineteenth-century defences of the Haven. It has now been converted into a hotel.

of fortifications were recommended, consisting of Thorn Island Fort, South Hook Fort and the strengthening of Stack Rock (to be enclosed within a curved casemated battery), together with Hubberston and Popton Forts. Building work at South Hook commenced in 1859. It had, like Hubberston, a D-shaped keep, caponiers covering the ditch, and was built to command Milford Haven and the Dale roads. The fort crossed fire with the equally impressive forts at Hubberston and Popton. Hubberston had, in addition to a somewhat earlier and open battery, twelve artillery casemates, but only eleven of these received armoured shields. Its roof was later given a concrete plinth to support Moncrieff pits, which were now replacing the casemated batteries – their elevated position, in this case, largely obviating the advantages of the disappearing carriage. Popton was started in 1859, with an irregular, hexagonal, small-bastioned barrack block and a casemated battery built of limestone and brick with a bombproof roof. Fort Scoveston was started two years later and was, with Chapel Bay Battery,

West Blockhouse, Milford Haven: now owned by the Landmark Trust, this finely built fort formed part of the defences of Milford Haven.

one of the two new Milford Haven land fortifications proposed and actually built in accordance with the Royal Commission's proposals. It was originally intended to stand in a line of five forts to block the eastern approaches to the Haven but it now stands isolated, the other forts never having been built. Scoveston was never armed. In the First World War it was used to house troops manning local anti-invasion works. The Commission also made recommendations concerning the need to protect potential landing-places, but only the fort on Saint Catherine's Island at Tenby was built. In 1866 the forts played their part in the 'M H Experiment' to test the effectiveness of the combination of mines, coastal artillery and searchlights to defend a commercial port. The attackers failed to penetrate the defences.

In 1867 Lieutenant Colonel Jervois, Deputy Director of Fortifications, investigated the progress of the work on the defences of the haven and found that Stack Rock Fort, South Hook Fort, Hubberston Battery, Popton Battery and Fort Scoveston were all in various stages of completion. All of the coastal batteries were practically complete apart from Chapel Bay, where the final plan had not been approved. In the final plan of 1870–7 it emerged as a rectangular, low-profile battery enclosed by an earthen rampart, with a *chemin des rondes* and a ditch containing a 16 foot (4.9 metre) high wall. Four concrete bombproof casemates and a master gunner's cottage provided the accommodation; two caponiers covered the ditch. With work not starting until the 1890s, it would represent a transitional design, incorporating old and new features. Its 1905 armament consisted of three 6 inch (152 mm) guns and three Maxim machine-guns. In the Second World War it served as a mine-observation post.

Most of the fortifications would be substantially modified during their construction, especially Stack Rock Fort, with its new, tiered and casemated circular battery. It was originally designed to have two tiers of guns but only one level was so equipped, the other tier being used as barrack space. The area's required garrison in times of war was calculated to be up to eight thousand men, and over three hundred guns would be required to arm the forts and batteries – although the numbers varied considerably during the lifespan of the fortifications.

The majority of the works were complete by the early 1870s but, as we have seen, developments in artillery were rendering fortifications of this type obsolete. The technological changes led to the remodelling of batteries, that at Chapel Bay being considerably altered over a relatively short period of time. The fortifications at Milford Haven were largely superseded by the proposals of the Stanhope Committee of 1904, two 9.2 inch (234 mm) batteries being built at the mouth of the Haven at South Hook Fort and East Blockhouse. In the Second World War a number of emergency batteries were built, including the fine, surviving Soldiers' Rock Battery at Milford Haven, commanded in 1940 by Major Tom Hitchens RA.

The Milford Haven area is one of the few defended ports in which the fortifications are all generally of one period, the majority being constructed within a period of twenty years. Each work shows considerable differences in design, together with individual and distinctive features, and most were designed to be mutually supporting.

Tyneside

In the nineteenth century this region's prosperity had been built on coal-mining and heavy industry. It also contained important shipyards and the armament works of W. G. Armstrong at Elswick. The company had been pioneers in the introduction of breech-loading artillery in 1855. Elswick was the only place in the world in which warships were both built and armed locally. In 1877 the Defence Committee reported that the area was of the highest commercial importance and was fortuitously provided with naturally commanding positions for defence on either side of the River Tyne. Tynemouth Castle commanded entry to the Tyne with its battery, although little modernisation had taken place since the time of the Napoleonic Wars. The Committee proposed a new armament of 11 inch (279 mm) and 10 inch (254 mm) rifled muzzle-loaders together with the submarine mining of the mouth of the river and a new battery at Sunderland. However, little was done. In 1893 there were 6 inch (152 mm) disappearing guns installed at Tynemouth Castle and one of the same size at Spanish Battery, as well as a number of quick-firing guns at both sites. In 1901 the new MkVII 6 inch coast gun with a range of 12,000 yards (11,000 metres), together with the 9.2 inch (234 mm) MkX gun with a range of 29,200 yards (26,700 metres), replaced the earlier guns. Spanish Battery also received the new 6 inch gun, whilst Frenchman's Point Battery received examples of both guns.

In 1905 the region's defences were reappraised, as it was now felt that the area was 'unlikely to be attacked by heavy vessels', and some downgrading took place. This decision was reversed the year before the outbreak of the First World War: the level of protection required was now deemed to be commensurate with that of a principal naval base. This was because of the growing importance of the region's shipbuilding (30 per cent of naval shipping at that time was built on the Tyne) and armaments industries. Despite this, little was done apart from the rehabilitation of the 9.2 inch (234 mm) guns mothballed in 1905 and the digging of trenches against a possible enemy landing at the outbreak of war. The bombardment of Whitby, Scarborough and Hartlepool by the German High Seas Fleet in December 1914 highlighted the vulnerability of the eastern coast of Britain. Heugh Battery at Hartlepool had returned fire, scoring hits on the heavy cruiser *Blücher*. Rail-mounted guns were rushed to the area, the guardship HMS *Illustrious* was moored in the Tyne, and the minefield was re-established. Two 4.7 inch (119 mm) quick-firing guns were installed at New Roker Battery at Sunderland in 1916, together with a new 6 inch (152 mm) battery at Blyth to prevent enemy landings on this stretch of coast and to act as an examination battery. Despite these emergency works the area was still felt to be vulnerable to long-range bombardment. In 1916 the navy offered the War Office two of the twin-gun turrets from HMS *Illustrious*. The offer was accepted and two sites were chosen for each of the Tyne turrets (with a range of 24,500 yards; 22,400 metres): at Hartley on the north of the Tyne and at Marsden on south Tyneside. Both batteries were named after distinguished generals – Kitchener and Roberts respectively. The long range of the guns enabled the towns of Blyth and Sunderland and the River Tyne to be covered. However, there were problems to be solved in the installation of this unusual armament. The magazines, the engines for power and the crew quarters were 30 feet (9.1 metres) below ground level, only the turrets being visible above ground level. Begun in 1917, the two batteries remained unfinished at the end of the war. Finally completed in 1921, the turrets fired twelve proof rounds but were thereafter put on a care and maintenance basis, later being broken up – although the director tower for the turrets does survive.

The River Forth defences

The earlier defences of this area consisted of Leith Fort of 1780 and the Leith Martello Tower of 1812. These defences were ineffective: the fort had been badly sited, and the tower had never been armed. Other defences existed or had existed at Inchcolm, Inchgarvie, Inchkeith, North Queensferry and Blackness Castle, but in the late nineteenth century the Forth was effectively defenceless. At the beginning of the twentieth century, however, the naval bases of Scotland had begun to assume a new importance. The centre of gravity of British naval defence had shifted north to meet the threat posed by Germany's High Seas Fleet, which operated out of the German North Sea ports. By the time of the First World War the Forth had progressed from being a defended commercial harbour and anchorage to an important naval port, becoming the anchorage for the defence of Britain in the North Sea.

The island of Inchkeith had long been the key to the defence of the Forth and had been fortified by the French under the Auld Alliance in the sixteenth century. All maritime traffic passed on either side of the island, but it was not until the latter part of the nineteenth century that the range of coastal artillery was sufficient to command both channels from land-based batteries located this far downstream. The development of the defences occurred between 1880 and 1910, when a system of inner and outer defence lines for the Forth was conceived and established. As the range of guns increased, the lines were repositioned, being pushed further forward to protect the anchorage. The Committee for Home Defence had earlier, in 1858, recommended the establishment of two heavy gun batteries at Inchkeith, crossing fire with a third at Kinghorn on the Fife coast. New defences were also recommended in Scotland at the Firth of Tay, the Moray Firth and at other lesser ports on the east coast. While there were plans in the 1860s for three forts on Inchkeith, nothing was done for almost twenty years apart from the purchase of land at Inchkeith and Kinghorn. However, in 1878 construction work did begin after increased tension with Russia, the Forth being seen as vulnerable to attack from north-eastern European ports. Navvies worked for fourteen hours a day, six days a week, to complete the defences. South Fort, West Fort and East Fort now crossed fire with the 10 inch (254 mm) rifled muzzle-loaders at Kinghorn. Contemporary commentators were impressed with the forts, skilfully blending into the landscape, the only objects visible being the guns themselves. Some of the works, overlooked by higher ground, were believed to be vulnerable to landing parties and it was felt that the combined total of six rifled muzzle-loaders might be insufficient to defend either channel against a determined attack by warships.

The Morley Committee in 1882 proposed a package of measures to improve the Forth, Clyde, Tay and Aberdeen defences. At the Forth an inner line of defences at the Queensferries led now to protection by a line of inner and outer defences. Effective protection was delayed until the Inchkeith–Kinghorn line had been strengthened with the new 9.2 inch (234 mm) breech-loading gun emplaced between the lighthouse and East Fort. A further report in 1894 stated that the Forth was now vulnerable to attack by the new cruiser warship. The result was four new batteries at the Queensferries: Carlingnose, Coastguard, Dalmeny and Inchgarvie. The provision of submarine mining was undertaken in the 1880s: this was a potent method of defence as it induced caution in the attacker, as well as bringing about his destruction. The American Civil War had demonstrated its effectiveness. A Royal Engineers and Royal Artillery report of 1887 pointed to the need to defend the new Forth Railway Bridge, this being an important line of communication, together with the protection of the area above the Queensferries for possible use by the fleet in a future war. The well-preserved Braefoot Battery was one of a number built along the shores of the Forth, consisting of an inner line of batteries grouped to protect the Forth Railway Bridge together with the batteries around the Queensferries. It conformed to the Forth defence scheme of 1905, requiring protection against an attack by cruisers and motor torpedo boats on the docks, shipping, and the defences of Rosyth. By 1914 there were three lines of batteries, including the new middle line at Hound Point, Downing Point and Braefoot. The last of these was armed in 1915 with two 9.2 inch (234 mm) guns, which were transported by train. The guns were then conveyed by steam tractor from the train to the new battery, which also had its own pier, defensible barracks, blockhouse, pillboxes and barbed wire defences. The battery was to be short-lived, however, being decommissioned in 1917. Other twentieth-century island and shore batteries protecting the Forth were located at Leith, Cramond, Inchmickery and Inchgarvie.

The River Clyde defences

Being on the western side of Britain, facing away from Europe, the Clyde was not felt to be as vulnerable as eastern or southern ports and harbours. Dumbarton Castle was armed with guns and there was an early-nineteenth-century battery at Greenock. New batteries were built in the 1880s following the recommendations of the 1882 Morley Committee, and in the First World War a battery for two 9.2 inch (234 mm) guns was built at Gourock. In the Second World War the Clyde was a vital war harbour and shipbuilding centre, protected by existing and emergency batteries.

Orkney

The main anchorage of the fleet in both world wars was at Scapa Flow and therefore the protection of this anchorage might be considered to have been vital. By 1910 Germany had overtaken France as the potential enemy. The Home Ports Defence Committee had visited the area in 1912 and a scheme of defence had been drawn up – but nothing was done, mainly because there was a lack of co-operation between the Admiralty and the War Office. Earlier defences had existed on Orkney in the form of the two Hackness Martello Towers and the battery at Longhope, although at the beginning of the twentieth century local batteries were still using the obsolete rifled muzzle-loaders. The Grand Fleet moved to the Scapa anchorage in 1914, but the anchorage possessed no guns to protect it. Weapons were removed quickly from warships to protect the entrances to the anchorage. Had Germany known of this weakness she could have mounted a devastating attack by fast destroyers. Later in the war a number of 6 inch (152 mm) and 4 inch (102 mm) guns from ex-United States stocks were emplaced, manned by Royal Marines, to give additional cover to the entrances. The fleet returned to Scapa Flow at the outbreak of war in 1939. However, the anchorage was only slightly better defended then than it had been in 1914. Again, guns had to be moved from ships into improvised positions for land defence. In October 1939 HMS *Royal Oak* was sunk by a U-boat that had slipped unnoticed into the Flow, and there were also air attacks on other ships. The fleet retreated to the relative safety of the west coast of Scotland pending the updating of the defences, which included the building of two 6 inch (152 mm) batteries and causeways to block the entrances to Scapa Flow. The modern twin 6 pounder anti-motor-torpedo-boat ordnance, designed originally for use in Singapore, was installed in nine locations from the autumn of 1941 to give much-needed protection against fast attack craft.

THE LONDON DEFENCE SCHEME

The development of modern rail networks and, in 1886, the possibility of a Franco-Russian naval alliance threatening the supremacy of the Royal Navy introduced the alarming prospect of the rapid mobilisation of a continental army and its rushing by steamboat across the English Channel. London was again vulnerable to an invasion. Unlike most European cities, London possessed no girdle of modern fortifications, apart from those few controlling access to the capital's river. To build a system similar

Henley Grove, Surrey: a mobilisation centre, its weakly defended entrance provided with a small number of rifle loopholes. The earthen banks protected the work and could, in an emergency, mount artillery.

Reigate, Surrey: a mobilisation centre on the North Downs, showing the interior with a store building to the left, together with its surrounding earthworks.

to that of, say, Portsmouth would have been prohibitively expensive, and in any event there was a mood developing against these monumentally expensive and inflexible works. General Sir Edward Hamley suggested surrounding the capital with a ring of entrenched positions to be manned by the Volunteers, leaving the field army free to attack an invader on the beaches. A similar system of fieldworks and positions for artillery and infantry was to be developed at Twydall near Chatham in the late 1880s. In 1886 Major Elsdale produced a paper suggesting a system of quickly dug earthworks for artillery and infantry backed up by built magazines at intervals of 5 miles (8 km). The National Defence Act of 1888 led to eight new battleships being ordered to placate the 'Blue Water School', but the Secretary of State for War also agreed to the building of earthwork fortifications to block any enemy advance from the south and east towards London. In 1889 Colonel Ardagh, with a small committee, worked out the finer details, the works being completed by 1892.

The London Defence Scheme emerged as a 70 mile (113 km) defence line running along the escarpment of the North Downs, then swinging north, crossing the Thames, and resuming in Essex. The fieldworks would not be constructed until an emergency, but a number of small forts, called mobilisation centres, were established as storage facilities. Provided with a caretaker and his cottage, they were generally sited at strategic gaps through which communications routes ran. Thirteen sites were chosen for the centres: at Pewley Hill, Henley Grove, Denbies, Box Hill, Betchworth, Reigate, West Merstham, Fosterdown, Woldingham, Betsoms Hill, Halstead, Farningham and North Weald. These low and well-camouflaged miniature forts of earth and concrete were protected by a Twydall Profile but possessed relatively weak gorge defences. Although modestly defensible, the forts were primarily designed to hold artillery, ammunition and stores such as tools in order that, in a national emergency, fieldworks for infantry and artillery could be dug with rapidity. Those positions in an especially commanding situation also contained terrepleins with protective traverses for the mounting, in an emergency, of an artillery battery, using the wheeled ordnance that they stored. Others were solely infantry positions of a semicircular form, some with a loopholed wall at the gorge. The largest of the thirteen, Fort Halstead, was a miniature version of some of the Chatham forts, with

Hurst Castle, Hampshire: a 38 ton 12.5 inch (317 mm) rifled muzzle-loader on a metal, traversing carriage. Above the gun are various tools, including a long-handled sponge and auger used to clean out the barrel in order to remove any remaining combustible material after firing. The other implement is the ramrod. The small trolley contains a Palliser shell.

its ditches revetted in concrete. The fort, presumably because of its secure situation, was used during the Cold War in connection with Britain's nuclear weapons research. The military life of the mobilisation centres was short and all except Fort Halstead were sold in 1907, at which time the belief had revived that the Royal Navy was supreme and that, therefore, invasion was an unlikely prospect.

SUMMARY

The end of the nineteenth century and the beginning of the twentieth brought in new concepts: large, costly and inflexible fortifications were now considered to be thoroughly out of date. The future lay in cheaper, more rapidly built, dispersed and better camouflaged coastal defence batteries constructed of earth and concrete. The range and type of artillery were also rationalised. An 1899 artillery manual recorded that there were still in service nineteen different calibres of breach and rifled muzzle-loading, quick-firing and smooth-bore ordnance on a multiplicity of

Dunree Hill Battery, Donegal: although now in the Republic of Ireland, this British, late-nineteenth-century 6 inch (152 mm) breech-loading battery is representative of the many built at this time for coastal and harbour defence. Ammunition was stored in separate underground magazines on either side of the gun. Ready-use lockers were placed around the base of the gun pit.

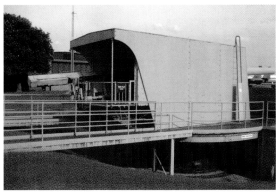

The 9.2 inch (233 mm) was the largest of the new generation of coastal artillery guns introduced at the end of the nineteenth century. The gun illustrated here originally formed part of the defences of Gibraltar and is now at the Imperial War Museum, Duxford, Cambridgeshire. The top photograph shows the breech (left) and its loading mechanism, while below is the massive central pivot on which the gun turned. The railings were not part of the gun's original equipment. The lower photograph shows the front of the turret and the barrel, together with the substantial concrete apron designed to protect the gun and its pivot.

carriages. By 1905 this had been reduced to just four calibres of breech-loading artillery: 9.2 inch (234 mm), 6 inch (152 mm), 4.7 inch (119 mm) and 12 pounder quick-firing. In the early 1890s there occurred the first comprehensive rearmament of Britain's coastal defences since the Royal Commission report of 1860. Important developments were also taking place in fire-control systems with the introduction of rangefinders and telecommunication systems. The information from the Watkins depression rangefinders and position finders could now be relayed directly to the guns

Edinburgh Castle: smoothbore breech-loaders of the nineteenth century on cast-iron garrison carriages. To the left of the stone sentry box is the Noonday gun.

A 3.7 inch (85 mm) heavy anti-aircraft gun. Although this gun is incorrectly mounted in a coastal artillery gun pit at Fort Paull, East Yorkshire, rather than in a heavy anti-aircraft battery emplacement, the photograph gives a good indication of a 3.7 inch gun on a static mounting and of its crew at 'action stations'. The loader is at the rear while one gunner moves the gun and its platform and the other elevates the gun.

by telegraph. The introduction of the autosight on the gun's cradle gave gunners the opportunity to control their guns over shorter ranges. Hitherto, the control of the guns had been problematic as the officer in charge often had to direct fire from a position well away from the smoke of the guns. The mixture of old rifled muzzle-loaders, a few breech-loaders and some quick-firing guns in the Thames, for example, was representative of coastal defence in the 1890s. The rifled muzzle-loaders were now

The breech end of a 6 inch (152 mm) coastal artillery gun, Newhaven Fort, East Sussex. The breechblock (A) is opened by swinging the lever (B), and the shell and a bagged charge in a fabric bag are inserted into the barrel (C). The breech is then closed. The firing mechanism consisted of a cartridge fitted into the centre of the block at D and ignited by a striker initiated by pulling on a lanyard; this ignited the bagged cordite charge. The gun's recoil was reduced by the two pneumatic cylinders located below the breech at E. The elevation and movement of the gun and its platform (F) were controlled by the controls at G, behind the protective shield (H). By the shield is the gun sight (I). When the gun had been fired it was necessary to sponge out the interior of the barrel to ensure that no burning fragments of the charge remained.

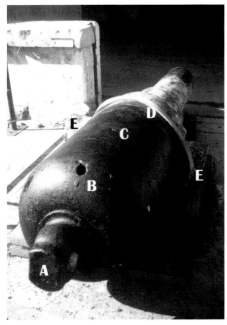

The barrel of a rifled muzzle-loading gun. The gun has seen post-military service as a bollard for the mooring of ships. A is the cascable: ropes would have been passed through the circular opening for the hoisting of the barrel into fortifications using a block and tackle. The opening also served as a means, by ropes and pulleys, for the movement of the gun and its carriage when in position in a fortification. B are holes for the fitting of sights for the aiming of the gun. C is the vent for the fitting of an igniter mechanism for the gunpowder charge. D is the royal crest. E are the trunnions which would have rested in grooves on the gun carriage. The trunnions enabled the barrel to be elevated or depressed when on the carriage.

obsolete against the naval breech-loaders of the continental powers but rearmament with more modern weapons such as the new 6 inch (152 mm) gun had been slow. Over the next ten years most of the muzzle-loaders were withdrawn. With the new generation of guns it was now possible to achieve ranges in excess of 6 miles (10 km): in 1905 the breech-loading guns at Grain and Sheerness in Kent could cover the approaches to both the Thames and the Medway. (Artillery towers remained in use well into the nineteenth century, for example those at Pembroke Dock.) The sea forts represented the ultimate development of the large round guntowers, these and the other massive works of the Royal Commission eventually being rendered obsolete by ever more powerful guns. In future, concealment and dispersal would be the norm in coastal batteries.

An example of one of the new generation of quick-firing guns built to deal with the threat of fast motor torpedo boats and motor gunboats. This example is a 6 pounder of 1898 at Tilbury Fort, Essex. Behind it are two models of the 12 pounder quick-firing gun.

8
The world wars

Throughout much of the nineteenth century France had been seen as the prime potential enemy to Britain. At the beginning of the following century Germany was seen to be the emerging threat, evidenced by her scramble for African colonies and her growing and powerful navy. The signing of the Entente Cordiale between Britain and France in 1904 isolated Germany as the new and sole threat. Turn of the century literature, for example *The Invasion* by William le Queux and *The Riddle of the Sands* by Erskine Childers, popularised the fear of a German invasion. This threat became even greater on the outbreak of war in 1914, with the early bombardment of several English east-coast ports by the German High Seas Fleet: if Germany could get this close to Britain, then the prospect of an invasion was more than fictional romancing. While the Royal Navy remained the principal deterrent to invasion, it was becoming clear that its continuing overseas commitments meant that it could no longer guarantee the security of the English Channel. Coastal batteries would, with the fieldworks and pillboxes built in the south and east of England, form the basis of the country's anti-invasion measures. The last circular sea forts were built at Bull Sand and Haile Sand during the war to protect the port of Hull, facing the North Sea.

London was again considered to be vulnerable. A Thames and Medway defence plan had been drawn up before the First World War and at the outbreak of war this was put into action with the building of trenches and pillboxes, the preparation of artillery positions and the laying of barbed wire to form a number of defence lines, for example one that followed a line from Ongar to Epping in Essex. The intention of the defences was to hold up the invader until the main central force arrived to repel

Renney Battery, Plymouth: one of the First World War infantry blockhouses for the landward defence of this 9.2 inch (234 mm) battery.

Bull Sand Fort is one of two forts built to guard the mouth of the Humber off Spurn Head. It was not completed until 1919. Its principal armament was four 6 inch (152 mm) roof-mounted guns. Searchlights were positioned around its walls.

him – a policy repeated in 1940 by General Ironside. Defence schemes were also drawn up for the protection of the eastern coast and other areas of England. During the emergency a number of the small defence posts that we now call pillboxes (named after the small cylindrical cardboard boxes in which pills were once dispensed) were built. Some still survive, such as those covering the crossings of the River Ant defence line in Norfolk and built in pairs for mutual defence. Three distinct designs were used in East Anglia: a circular, concrete position with an overhanging roof; a larger design made of concrete blocks; and one that was hexagonal and of poured concrete, resembling the more commonly seen Second World War designs. These were provided with steel doors and loophole shutters. The building of pillboxes as a means of anti-invasion defence carried on until the last year of the war. Underwater minefields were also established across river mouths and harbours, for example that controlled by Coalhouse Fort close to the Thames in Essex; the fort also contained an examination battery for the firing of warning shots at shipping that failed to respond to signals to hove-to. Coalhouse Fort also played a part in the air defence of London against German bombers and airships, supporting a battery of 3 inch (76 mm) anti-aircraft guns. Even earlier fortifications were still in use for military purposes – the grim gatehouse of Richmond Castle in Yorkshire, for example, serving as a prison for conscientious objectors.

On 11th November 1918 the 'war to end all wars' came to an end. Although great swathes of Belgium, northern and eastern France and eastern Europe had been ravaged and the German population had been reduced to virtual starvation, the soil of Britain had suffered relatively little damage. Anticipating a lasting continental peace, the British armed forces, although stretched by the responsibilities of protecting the

Greatstone, Kent: one of the sound mirrors built on the south and east coasts of England.

Empire, were reduced and allowed to stagnate. One threat was recognised, however: the growing menace of bomber aircraft, making their first appearance in the First World War, led to the need for an earlier warning of their approach. A number of concrete sound mirrors were therefore built along the south-east and eastern coasts of England from the First World War to detect aircraft and airships crossing the English Channel. With Germany beaten, the only likely continental threat was Britain's First World War ally, France. Rapidly made obsolete by ever-faster aircraft and the development of radar, a group of these concrete, sculptural structures survives at Greatstone in Kent.

The rise of fascism in the 1930s and the aggressive stance of Germany and Italy in the Spanish Civil War, in which their weapons and tactics were honed and perfected, along with the annexation by Hitler of Austria and Czechoslovakia, created alarm in the late 1930s. Britain began to rearm and new anti-aircraft defences were prepared, but the regular army was still weak and unprepared for a further European war. There had, however, been some developments in coastal artillery in the period between the wars. A 'fortress system' was introduced in the 1930s and a chain of observation posts was established along the coastline. Data from the posts was sent to a local plotting room that transmitted the ranges and bearings of ships to the batteries, which might not have had initial visual contact with their targets. The system was supplemented in the Second World War by the arrival of coast defence radar that could 'see' in all light and weather conditions.

On 1st September 1939 Germany invaded Poland. France and Britain, obligated by treaty to the defence of Poland, declared war, but not until two days later. The swiftness of the German victory meant that there was little that Britain or her ally France could do to help Poland – even if there had been a realistic plan of aid by the allies. Although Hitler had planned to attack France next, the attack did not take place until May 1940, after a successful but costly, in shipping terms, invasion of Norway. Following the brilliant Blitzkrieg campaign by Germany, France, whose army in the 1930s had been held to be invincible, declared an armistice on 22nd June 1940. Britain was left on her own, but only after losing part of her sovereignty following the German occupation of the Channel Islands in the same year. The Germans turned the islands, especially Alderney, into a fortress, although they were never to be totally integrated into the Atlantic Wall. In fortifying the islands the Germans often made use of earlier fortifications such as those built by Jervois on Alderney in the nineteenth century. The Germans put into effect a large number of different designs of fortification for the many different types of armament installed in the Channel Islands and along the continental Atlantic Wall.

Britain, having left behind most of the heavier weapons of the British Expeditionary Force in France – especially anti-tank guns, was now facing a confident and, so far, unbeaten enemy. Although before the fall of France Churchill had posed the question

Fairbourne, Gwynedd: anti-tank obstacles, together with a small hexagonal pillbox of the War Office FW3/22 pattern, cover this beach.

of what would happen if significant numbers of German troops were able to land on British soil, apart from certain of the more important ports such as Dover, Britain's land defences had received little attention. The Germans, from the Pas de Calais, were now in sight of the English coast and, with aircraft and super-heavy artillery, could bombard the south of England in preparation for invasion. Super-heavy guns

Fort Clonque, Alderney: a representative view of one of the many German fortifications on the Channel Islands, in this case a casemated gun position (for a captured French 105 mm [4.1 inch] gun) within the walls of Jervois's picturesque fort. The German occupiers called the site, appropriately, 'Resistance Nest Steinfeste'.

Eckington, Worcestershire: a prefabricated 'Stent' pillbox forming part of the River Avon stopline. Some form of camouflage would have been applied in 1940 to make it less obvious.

were moved into position along the coast of Kent, leading to ineffectual artillery duels with their more powerful German rivals in the Pas de Calais. Canal and other shallow-draught craft now began to be gathered together by the Germans in ports along the French, Belgian and Dutch coasts, inviting the attention of the Royal Air Force. While the Royal Navy would again remain the principal deterrent to seaborne invasion, British land defences received urgent and frantic attention. The possibility of airborne landings led to the defence of airfields by anti-aircraft guns, as well as the construction of infantry earthworks and concrete pillboxes: if the enemy could seize

Wootton Rivers, Kennet and Avon Canal, Wiltshire: a large anti-tank gun emplacement on the GHQ Line designed to take the 2 pounder anti-tank gun, which could be fired from one of two open positions. It is likely that sandbags were used to cover the opening not protected by the gun's shield.

Coalhouse Fort, Essex: a Second World War XDO (extended defence officer's) post from which the local Thames underwater minefield was controlled.

airfields, as had happened in Norway in 1940, it would be possible for him to fly in troops and supplies. The defence of ports and the coastline was similarly addressed by the sowing of mines, the building of pillboxes, barbed-wire entanglements, roadblocks, counter-bombardment and emergency coastal batteries – and even flame defences. Commons, beaches, wide roads and even reservoirs were obstructed to prevent the enemy's transport aircraft and floatplanes from landing. In effect the whole of Britain would become a fortress.

The most pressing problem, however, was how to deal with the enemy – especially his tanks – should he land and penetrate the thinly spread coastal defences. In the late summer and autumn of 1940, because of the grave loss of war *matériel* in France, Britain's army faced the enemy with few and inadequate anti-tank defences. Where the enemy might make his landing was also unknown, and so a nationwide system of inland anti-tank stoplines was put in place by the Commander-in-Chief of Home Forces, General Ironside. What reserves of men and equipment were available were husbanded behind the coast so as to be rushed to the invasion areas in requisitioned buses and coaches. The principal stopline was the War Office General Headquarters Line, protecting the approaches to London and the Midlands, Britain's principal manufacturing region. In addition there were a number of Army Command and Corps stoplines, the whole splitting the countryside into massive anti-tank 'corrals'. Important cities and ports were provided with rings of defences: Liverpool, for example, had to have two rings on either side of the River Mersey as the 1930s Mersey Tunnel now provided a direct approach route from the west. London, as the capital city, was surrounded by several rings of anti-invasion defences. The stoplines often made use of existing features such as canals and rivers as anti-tank obstacles, together with miles of specially dug anti-tank ditches. The pillbox re-emerged, armed with infantry weapons and anti-tank guns and sited to prevent the infiltration of infantry and tanks across the stoplines at crossing points that were not intended for demolition: it was necessary to keep open certain points to launch counter-attacks against the invader. Other pillboxes were built to protect airfields, heavy anti-aircraft, radar and searchlight sites, factories, and government installations. A number of pillbox designs had been circulated by the War Office to army commands at the time of the fall of France, the most common remaining examples being those built to the Fortifications and Works drawing numbers 22 and 24. A bewildering range of unofficial pillbox designs can also still be seen around Britain.

The nineteenth-century forts still had a part to play. At Coalhouse Fort, for example, two 5.5 inch (140 mm) ex-naval guns, part of the nationwide emergency battery system, were positioned in protected gun houses on the roof of the nineteenth-century artillery casemates. As part of the anti-invasion measures the fort was converted

Pevensey Castle, East Sussex: a Second World War loophole (right foreground), one of several built into the Roman and medieval fabric.

into a modern defended area with Spigot mortars and wire entanglements. The fort again controlled a minefield and also served as a degaussing (the system of making shipping impervious to magnetic mines) checkpoint for ships leaving the port of London. Nearby was the Bowaters Farm heavy anti-aircraft gun site, which in August 1939 had mobile 3.7 inch (94 mm) guns, replaced in 1940 by the turreted 4.5 inch (114 mm) gun, and latterly the radar-controlled 5.25 inch (133 mm) dual-purpose gun. At Portsmouth, beneath the bulk of Fort Southwick on Portsdown Hill, was the Combined Underground Operations Centre, first put to use during the Dieppe raid of August 1942. In June 1944 it was the headquarters of Admiral Ramsay, who was in charge of the naval armada that on 6th June 1944 sailed for the Normandy coast. Ramsay had lived a similar troglodytic existence in June 1940 whilst directing Operation Dynamo, the evacuation from Dunkirk, in tunnels beneath Dover Castle.

The need for bombproof accommodation led to other adaptations: heavily reinforced cellars in Whitehall formed the Cabinet War Rooms, and a similar arrangement was used for the headquarters of Western Approaches in Liverpool. A number of Army Commands created underground battle headquarters, such as the one contained behind a chalk quarry face at Reigate in Surrey for Southern Command. For the civilian population reinforced cellars, the steel Anderson and brick communal air-raid shelters would have to make do.

During the late summer and autumn of 1940 the invasion period came and went, and in the winter Britain reviewed its defences. It had been realised at the end of the year that the effort in building over twenty thousand pillboxes had been a mistake: they were now considered to have been too vulnerable and wasteful of resources. From 1941 onwards Britain's anti-invasion policy moved towards a nationwide and intricate system of defended localities: this had formed a minor part of the previous summer's defences in the guise of defended 'nodal points'. The almost two million men of the Home Guard, gradually armed with relatively modern weapons, mainly from United States stocks, would now take over the defence of Britain, leaving the

High Ercall airfield, Shropshire: an airfield defence pillbox camouflaged to resemble a small building. Note the white-painted 'window surround' of the machine-gun embrasure and the false roof.

regular army to become increasingly involved with overseas campaigns. Existing pillboxes were retained where these fitted local defence plans – even if this involved using them as decoys to draw the enemy's fire. Small trench systems often known as weapons pits, and frequently of an arrowhead shape reminiscent of the bastion, combined with anti-tank roadblocks, flame traps and minefields, formed the nation's defences from 1941. Home Guard sub-artillery, such as the Smith Gun, Northover Projector or 29 mm (1.1 inch) Spigot mortar, and later the army's obsolete 2 pounder anti-tank gun, were readied for emplacement in ambush positions. These simpler strong points might consist of hedges reinforced with barbed wire or stout buildings, often houses, reinforced with sandbags and barbed wire in order to convert them into strong points. An Englishman's home would now, literally, become his castle!

Airfield defences were revised according to a system of priorities. From 1941 onwards most would have their own concrete and bombproof battle headquarters as well as other existing or additional hardened defences or fieldworks. The constant fear was that in an invasion German airborne forces might attempt to capture an airfield and then bring in supplies to expand their front: this would happen at Crete in 1941. Airfields were also considered to be especially vulnerable points as they held the precious supplies of aircraft and spare parts so vital to fight the war.

Despite the building of large numbers of anti-aircraft batteries, there was a concern that ever faster-flying Luftwaffe bombers could approach the important ports of Liverpool and London from the sea and avoid the cities' anti-aircraft defences. At the request of the Admiralty (which was responsible for the defence of the sea approaches) the engineer Guy Maunsell designed an anti-aircraft sea fort to protect the Thames estuary. The first example was placed in position in February 1942 and

Sutton Weaver, Cheshire: one of almost forty heavy anti-aircraft sites protecting the Mersey area in the Second World War. However, the structures in the photograph, although resembling those built during the war, are believed to date from the early Cold War period when there was an upgrading of a number of wartime sites situated in especially strategic locations. On the right is one of the 3.7 inch (94 mm) emplacements.

fitted with 3.7 inch (94 mm) anti-aircraft guns, radar, searchlights and 40 mm (1.6 inch) Bofors light anti-aircraft guns. The Mersey forts were designed next and, although built by the navy, they were manned by the army, which required a greater spacing of the guns, hence they were of a different design to the navy's forts. The Mersey forts never fired a shot in anger and were demolished after the war. The guns and radar of those in the Thames – and here examples of the army forts were also positioned – played an important role in the battle against the V1 'Doodlebug' flying bombs in 1944.

Let us look at the development of a defended industrial area in the twentieth century. On Tyneside the Tynemouth Castle and Spanish Batteries on mobilisation in 1938 were ready for action. In 1939 two 6 inch (152 mm) emergency batteries were placed at Blyth and at Sunderland. The Blyth Old and Roker Batteries also were reinstated to mount 6 inch guns. Emergency batteries, often using surplus ex-naval guns, were sited at Berwick-upon-Tweed and Amble, with additional batteries at Blyth, Whitby and Seaham covering potential landing grounds or ports that might be a target for capture. On the beaches between Berwick-upon-Tweed and Seaham, in addition to beach defences of wire, concrete obstacles, anti-boat scaffolding, pillboxes and trenches, twenty-four Hotchkiss improvised 6 pounder anti-tank guns in pillboxes, together with three 4 inch (102 mm) anti-invasion guns, covered potential landing points. Protection for the emergency batteries increased after 1940 with the building of concrete gun houses around the guns, providing overhead and lateral cover, together with more permanent shelters for the crews and magazines.

Radar for the control of the gun batteries, along with the centralised fortress control system, organised by a fire commander, improved the potential of the batteries. However, there was only one heavy 9.2 inch (234 mm) gun in the area – that at Tynemouth Castle – for counter-bombardment work, supplemented in 1942 by 6 inch (152 mm) naval guns. In 1943 three 5.25 inch (133 mm) dual-purpose, radar-directed,

Freiston Shore, Lincolnshire: the gun house of the Boston examination battery. The holdfast bolts for securing the 6 inch (152 mm) gun remain in situ. The site also retains a number of the buildings of this 1940 emergency coastal battery: the building on the far left held a coastal-artillery searchlight.

turreted guns were emplaced at Park Battery. These had a range of 27,000 yards (24,700 metres) and represented the most up-to-date coastal defence system in the United Kingdom at that time. Like all other coastal defence batteries, Park Battery ceased to be operational on the standing down of coastal artillery in 1956.

The German invasion of the USSR in June 1941, coupled with the arrival of United States forces from 1942 onwards, had indicated that a German invasion was becoming less likely – and even less so after D-Day in June 1944. However, from that year relations with the Soviet ally began to deteriorate, culminating in Churchill's famous 'Iron Curtain' speech given in Fulton, Missouri, in March 1946.

9

The Cold War and the nuclear threat

The founding of the North Atlantic Treaty Organisation (NATO) in April 1949, the continued development of nuclear weapons by the eastern and western powers and the possibility of long-range Soviet aircraft and ground-launched nuclear missiles attacking NATO bases led to the establishment of American bases in Britain, turning the island into an 'unsinkable aircraft carrier'. The need to protect military and governmental organisations led to the development of new types of protected buildings. In the late 1940s and early 1950s Britain's aircraft early-warning radar system was overhauled under 'Operation Rotor'. In addition to new scanning equipment, a system of ground-control intercept and sector-operating centres was established in specially built reinforced concrete sunken or semi-sunken buildings. Because of the limited range of contemporary radar systems, a nationwide network of ground-controlled intercept hardened sites was required, those on the eastern side of Britain being sunken, those on the western side being semi-sunken. One of the largest east-coast sites was that at Anstruther in Fife, known as RAF Troywood: nearby were important military bases such as the Royal Air Force fighter station of Leuchars and the Rosyth naval dockyard, all requiring radar protection. To construct the sites, a hole up to 130 feet (40 metres) deep was excavated with a base layer of gravel to act as a gigantic shock absorber. A massive concrete shell, reinforced with tungsten rods, was then built, its exterior waterproofed with pitch and the interior

RAF Anstruther, Fife: the entrance, camouflaged to resemble a small house, gave access to the underground 'Rotor' radar bunker, later a Cold War Regional Government Headquarters.

Hack Green, Cheshire: a semi-sunken 'Rotor' radar bunker, with (left) an additional, protected generator building dating from its Regional Government Headquarters role in the Cold War.

lined with brick. A concrete raft in the backfilled earth above the bunker acted as a 'burster cap' to detonate bombs before they could hit the bunker proper. Entry into the sunken bunkers was via a building camouflaged to resemble a small house – a long sloping tunnel connecting with the underground centre. The west-coast, semi-sunken sites were entered directly at ground level. Air-conditioning and filters ensured that nuclear-contaminated air did not enter (although it appears that in the later use of such sites there was no protection for civilian staff against chemical or biological agents). The provision of generators, kitchens, dormitories and an independent water supply made the bunkers, in a period of emergency, self-sufficient for a considerable period of time.

To control the operation of Britain's anti-aircraft guns in the 1950s, a number of hardened gun-operations rooms were built. These were usually remote from the

Hack Green, Cheshire: a replica of the BBC broadcasting studio of the Cold War Regional Government Headquarters within the bunker.

3.7 inch (94 mm) or 5.25 inch (133 mm) batteries that they controlled, although the one at Elvaston in Derbyshire is close to a 3.7 inch battery. Other operations rooms made use of existing fortifications, for example the one at Crownhill Fort, Plymouth, and that beneath Dover Castle. Each contained a large plotting room with a viewing gallery for the control and direction of the guns against incoming targets. The reinforced-concrete, purpose-built rooms were said to be proof against a conventional 2000 pound (907 kg) bomb and also against earth tremor caused by a nearby nuclear explosion.

As radar systems developed in performance and missiles began to replace anti-aircraft artillery, the number of such bunkers was reduced and in the late 1950s, for example, RAF Anstruther became redundant. Within a few years, with the dropping of the first Soviet hydrogen bomb, a new role was found for this and the other redundant centres as Regional Seats of Government, and from the late 1960s as Regional Government Headquarters. In addition to the regional government centres, local authorities had their own protected war rooms underground: many police and most local authority headquarters in the 1960s had specially designed protected basements for civil defence purposes. The plan of central government was that in the event of a nuclear attack a bureaucracy would already be *in situ* in a protected and self-sufficient environment to administer the country, receiving instructions from the national government's underground headquarters. The three to four hundred personnel required to operate the headquarters in a national emergency were to be accommodated within the bunker, and so a massive refurbishment took place at Anstruther and at other locations. A variety of sites was chosen, such as a Second World War underground factory at Drakelow in Worcestershire, redundant 'Rotor' stations such as that at Hack Green in Cheshire, or in regional war rooms, and, again, in the tunnels beneath Dover Castle. Both the Secretary of State and Minister of State for Scotland were to be accommodated at Anstruther, along with their staffs and representatives of local government. The police and fire services, civil

Audlem, Cheshire: representative of many identical Cold War underground Royal Observer Corps monitor posts. The concrete steps lead up to the entrance hatch, and on the roof are the ventilator and also points for the attachment of monitoring instruments. It retains its original fence.

Londonderry, Northern Ireland: late-twentieth-century fortifications. These British Army observation posts are situated by the city walls and overlook the Republican area of Bogside. They are fitted with mesh screens as a precaution against blast bombs or rocket-propelled grenades.

defence, the Regional Commissioner, representatives from the armed forces and the BBC, for whom a small broadcasting studio was provided, were also represented. The breakdown of the communist bloc from 1989 onwards led to the end of the regional government headquarters system. A number are now open to public view, some have been demolished to make way for housing, while others are used as secure storage sites.

The Royal Observer Corps (ROC), which had played such an important role in the Second World War, was brought into the system of nuclear defence, forming the main component of the United Kingdom Warning and Monitoring Organisation (UKWMO). A network of underground monitoring posts, eventually numbering over fifteen hundred posts and thirty-one group headquarters, was built from 1957 onwards, although this number was to be halved following the 1968 defence cuts. The headquarters, located at ground level or semi-sunken, were capable of operating for one week under nuclear fall-out conditions with their own air-conditioning, emergency generator, catering and water supply and sleeping accommodation. The underground monitoring posts, with their crew of three ROC members, could also operate 'closed down' for one week. Their role was to report, by telephone, to their regional headquarters, the latter communicating with national government, on the fall of nuclear weapons. Externally mounted instruments fed information into the post, enabling the measurement of bomb characteristics; this information could predict the fall-out pattern, which, in theory, would be of value in the protection of the civilian population and would influence the military response. The UKWMO and the ROC were stood down, following the end of the Cold War, in 1992 but many of their posts survive, some preserved as small private museums.

The presence of NATO bases in Britain led to the appearance of a number of NATO standard military protected structures, such as those at Greenham Common in Berkshire that housed cruise missiles; other examples are the hardened aircraft shelters seen on Royal Air Force and United States Air Force airfields. Even

121

the humble pillbox reappeared in the form of the Yarnold Sangar, protecting the perimeters of military bases against possible terrorist attack. In Northern Ireland during the last three decades of the twentieth century police and military posts were fortified and observation posts were built in troubled areas such as Londonderry and along the border with the Republic of Ireland. These structures had to be protected against bullets, bombs and rocket-propelled grenades.

The fall of the Berlin Wall in the winter of 1989 led to the abandonment of many of the expensive defence systems of the Cold War. However, the possibility of terrorist attacks such as those on New York on 11th September 2001 and in London in July 2005 may well encourage the retention of the deepest existing structures, and even the construction of new underground and highly secret Government facilities.

Glossary

Apron: the protection of earth and concrete in front of a gun pit, designed to absorb the impact of shells landing close to a heavy gun.

Asdic: form of sonar equipment used to detect enemy submarines in the Second World War.

Bastion: work protruding from the main face of a fortification, usually in the form of an irregular pentagon.

Bastioned trace: a fortification having, in outline, walls with bastions protruding at regular intervals.

Boom defence: a barrier formed from a chain or cable and stretched across a waterway.

Caponier: small, single- or double-storeyed structure connected to the main work and provided with embrasures for cannon or musket so as to fire along the work's ditches.

Carnot wall: detached, low wall at the base of a rampart protecting the *chemin des rondes*.

Carronade: light, short-range artillery piece built by the Carron Company in the nineteenth century.

Casemate: vaulted chambers in a work containing gun positions, or used as barracks.

Chemin des rondes: a passageway, protected by a Carnot wall.

Counterscarp gallery: gallery for muskets or light cannon built into the outer face of a ditch; also used as a point from which to mount countermining operations.

Covered way: broad space on top of the outer face of the ditch, provided with a low wall for infantry fire into the field.

Culverin: early, light artillery piece.

Davit: small and simple crane used in nineteenth-century forts for the movement of ammunition from underground magazines to rampart gun positions.

En barbette: raised gun position on a parapet from where guns can fire over the parapet.

Enfilade: gunfire directed from end to end of a fortification.

Entrenchment: fortified area for the assembly of large bodies of troops.

Feste: nineteenth-century German system of fortification consisting of a group of irregular defences including long-range and close-support artillery and infantry.

Gabions: wicker baskets filled with earth or stones and used as a temporary field fortification.

Glacis: large, cleared area of sloping ground in front of a fortification.

Gorge: neck or interior side of a fortification.

HAA: heavy anti-aircraft (gun).

Haxo casemate: protected structure designed by Baron Haxo to house artillery pieces on the terreplein of a fortress.

Howitzer: wheeled artillery piece designed to fire shells at a high angle for plunging fire.

LAA: light anti-aircraft (gun).

Linstock: stick used to hold slow-burning cord and to light gunpowder in the touch-hole of a cannon.

Lunette: large detached work with flanks and an open gorge.

Machicolation: projecting gallery from which fire can be directed, especially at the area immediately below.

Magazine: room or rooms in a fort or battery used for the storage of shells and charges.

Mortar: short-range ordnance used to fire mortar bombs.

Petard: large charge of explosive placed in front of, typically, the gate of a fortress under siege in order to demolish the gate.

Places d'armes: protected positions adjacent to a fort for the assembly of troops, especially for the launch of counter-attacks.

Port war signal station: coastal position from which naval personnel can challenge shipping approaching a defended port.

Position finder cell: small emplacement on a battery for the mounting of instruments used to determine the range, position and speed of an enemy ship.

Rampart: the high bank on which the parapet stands.

Ravelin: triangular outwork placed in front of a curtain; if in front of the entrance to the work it would be crossed by bridges.

Redan: triangular bastion in advance of the main work.

Redoubt: small, detached stronghold without provision for flank defence.

Revetment: retaining wall in a ditch, built to retain the earth behind.

Salient: portion of a work that juts out into the field.

Sallyport: small gate in a stronghold giving on to its exterior and from which counter-attacks can be launched.

Sap: zigzag trench built by besiegers towards a besieged fortress.

Scarp: interior wall of a ditch.

Sconce: small, temporary star-shaped artillery fort of earth with a timber palisade.

Slight: to render a fortress indefensible.

Spigot mortar: Second World War anti-tank weapon, usually associated with the Home Guard.

Tenaille front: low-lying work placed between bastions to protect the lower portion of a curtain wall.

Terreplein: upper surface of a fortress on which artillery can be mounted.

Trace: plan of a fortification.

Traverse: large earthen bank built to protect portions of the interior of a fortress from enfilade fire.

Twydall Profile: light, defensive system developed at Twydall in Kent in the late nineteenth century.

Select gazetteer of fortifications open to the public

In addition to the sites listed below, it is possible to view the exteriors of many of the other surviving works mentioned in the text; however, privacy must be respected at all times.

The Landmark Trust (Shottesbrooke, Maidenhead, Berkshire SL6 3SW; telephone: 01628 825925; website: www.landmarktrust.org.uk) owns a number of works of fortification that are available for holiday letting. These include Crownhill Fort, Plymouth; the Martello Tower at Aldeburgh, Suffolk; West Blockhouse, Milford Haven; and Fort Clonque on Alderney.

Useful points of contact for checking opening times and other details are: Cadw, the Welsh heritage agency (Plas Carew, Unit 5/7 Cefn Coed, Parc Nantgarw, Cardiff CF15 7QQ; telephone: 01443 336000; website: www.cadw.wales.gov.uk); English Heritage (Customer Services Department, PO Box 569, Swindon SN2 2YP; telephone: 0870 333 1181; website: www.english-heritage.org.uk); the Environment and Heritage Service of Northern Ireland (Waterman House, 5-33 Hill Street, Belfast BT1 2LA; telephone: 028 9054 3145; website: www.ehsni.gov.uk); Historic Scotland (Longmore House, Salisbury Place, Edinburgh EH9 1SH; telephone: 0131 668 8600; website: www.historic-scotland.gov.uk). For information on fortifications on the Channel Islands the relevant tourist boards are Guernsey Tourist Board (PO Box 23, St Peter Port, Guernsey, Channel Islands GY1 3AN; telephone: 01481 723552; website: www.guernseytouristboard.com), Alderney Tourist Board (PO Box 1, Alderney GY9 3AA; telephone: 01481 822811; website: www.alderney. gov.gg) and Jersey Tourist Board (The Weighbridge, St Helier, Jersey JE2 3NF; telephone: 01534 633300; website: www.jerseyheritagetrust.org). For information specifically on the German defences of the Channel Islands refer to the Channel Islands Occupation Society's website: www.ciosjersey.org.uk (postal address: The Secretary, Les Geonnais de Bas, Rue des Geonnais, Vinchelez, St Ouen, Jersey JE3 2BS). Details of the fortifications of different periods to be found on the Isle of Man can be found on the website www.gov.im/tourism (postal address: Isle of Man Tourism, Sea Terminal Building, Douglas, Isle of Man IM1 2RG; telephone: 01624 686801). The database established by the Defence of Britain Project for Second World War sites can be accessed via the Council for British Archaeology's site, at www.britarch.ac.uk

ENGLAND
Berkshire
Donnington Castle, English Heritage (1 mile north of Newbury off the B4494). A late-fourteenth-century castle of which only the repaired gateway survives, but with well-preserved Civil War outer defences.

Kennet and Avon Canal. There are a considerable number of anti-invasion defences remaining along the line of the canal, part of the 1940 GHQ Line.

Cheshire
Chester city walls. Medieval city walls, with some Roman remains but showing Civil War damage, reinforcement and adaptation.

Fort Perch Rock (on the shore at New Brighton, close to the lighthouse). Telephone:

0151 630 2707. Built in the early nineteenth century to protect the entrance to the River Mersey and Liverpool, the fort, with its round corner towers and rampart-mounted cannon, presents a medieval appearance.

Hack Green Nuclear Bunker (from Audlem take the A525 Whitchurch road, taking a turn 1 mile west of Audlem, then a left turn 3 miles further along the road). Telephone: 01270 629219. Website: www.hackgreen.co.uk Semi-submerged Cold War Regional Government Headquarters.

Cornwall

Cromwell's Castle, English Heritage (on the west coast of Tresco, Isles of Scilly). A circular guntower of *c*.1650 guarding the anchorage of Bryher and Tresco.

Mount Edgcumbe Blockhouse (in Mount Edgcumbe Park), Cremyll, Torpoint, Cornwall PL10 1HZ. Telephone: 01752 822236. Website: www.mountedgcumbe. gov.uk. Small, square early artillery blockhouse.

Pendennis Castle, English Heritage (on Pendennis Head, 1 mile south-east of Falmouth). Artillery fortress of the time of Henry VIII, with central circular guntower and a later bastioned polygonal trace and gatehouse. A Second World War coastal artillery battery has also been preserved within the castle.

St Anthony Head, National Trust (at the southernmost point of the Roseland peninsula). Twentieth-century coastal gun battery with display boards.

St Catherine's Castle, English Heritage (1 mile south of Fowey on the west bank of Polruan harbour, reached via the South West Coast Path). Sixteenth-century blockhouse with adjacent Victorian battery.

St Mawes Castle, English Heritage (in St Mawes on the A3078). Telephone: 01326 270526. The most elaborately decorated of the artillery forts of Henry VIII: in the Second World War it supported a coastal defence battery.

Cumbria

Carlisle Castle, English Heritage (close to the city centre). Telephone: 01228 591922. A medieval fortress with sixteenth-century artillery works, it remained armed into the nineteenth century.

Devon

Bayards Cove Fort, English Heritage (in Dartmouth, on the river front). Small battery built at the beginning of the sixteenth century to protect Dartmouth harbour.

Berry Pomeroy Castle, English Heritage (2½ miles east of Totnes, off the A385). Telephone: 01803 866618. Late-fifteenth-century work in this medieval castle shows the provision of slits for handguns and a strengthened roof for artillery.

Crownhill Fort, Crownhill Fort Road, Plymouth PL6 5BX (on the A386 Plymouth to Tavistock road, 4 miles north of Plymouth city centre; follow signs to Crownhill, from which the fort is signposted). Telephone: 01752 793754. Website: www. crownhillfort.co.uk Probably the finest of Plymouth's Palmerston forts, it was provided with all-round defence and retains its original appearance.

Dartmouth Castle, English Heritage (1 mile south-east of Dartmouth, off the B3205). Telephone: 01803 833588. Artillery blockhouse of 1481 built to protect the harbour, with later, casemated battery.

Mount Batten (on a peninsula to the south-east of Plymouth, reached via the A379, Plymstock and Hooe). Telephone: 01752 404567. Cromwellian round artillery tower of the 1650s.

Royal Citadel Plymouth, English Heritage (at the eastern end of Plymouth Hoe). Guided tours only (contact: plymouthukbbg@hotmail.com). Bastioned fortress with baroque entrance designed in 1665 by Sir Bernard de Gomme.

Dorset

Corfe Castle, The Square, Corfe Castle, Wareham, Dorset BH20 5EZ. National Trust.

Telephone: 01929 481294. Medieval castle defended for the King in the Civil War, showing evidence of the substantial damage of the Parliamentarian slighting.

Nothe Fort, Barrack Road, Weymouth, Dorset DT4 8UF (on the easternmost point of Weymouth, overlooking the harbour). Telephone: 01305 766626. Website: www. fortressweymouth.co.uk A D-shaped casemated fort of the 1860s armed originally with ten heavy guns behind shields.

Portland Castle, English Heritage (overlooking Portland Harbour, in Castleton, on the Isle of Portland). Telephone: 01305 820539. Artillery fort of Henry VIII, built in 1540. Low, semicircular guntower together with segmental two-storey barracks.

Sherborne Old Castle, English Heritage (½ mile east of Sherborne, off the B3145). Telephone: 01935 812730. Evidence of the sixteen-day siege by Cromwell is visible in the form of bastioned earthworks protecting the entrance and other parts of this medieval castle.

Essex

Coalhouse Fort, East Tilbury, Essex RM18 8PB (reached via the A1013 Grays–Corringham road: take the minor road just before Stanford-le-Hope for East Tilbury and follow the road to the fort). Limited opening. Telephone: 01375 844203. Website: www.coalhousefort.co.uk 1860s casemated fort, part of the Thames defences.

Harwich Redoubt (located behind 29 Main Road, the B1352, close to the town centre). Telephone: 01255 503429. Website: www.harwich-society.com One of three circular redoubts built in the early nineteenth century, also containing a museum.

Kelvedon Hatch Secret Bunker, Crown Buildings, Kelvedon Hall Lane, Brentwood CM14 5TL. Telephone: 01277 364883. Website: www.japar.demon.co.uk Originally a Cold War RAF 'Rotor' radar station, then used for civil defence purposes, it ended its active life as a Regional Government Headquarters.

Tilbury Fort, English Heritage (½ mile east of Tilbury, reached off the A126). Telephone: 01375 858489. The finest example of a seventeenth-century bastioned fort in Britain.

Hampshire

Basing House, Redbridge Lane, Basing, Basingstoke, Hampshire RG24 7HB (1½ miles east of Basingstoke centre, on the northern side of Basingstoke Common). Telephone: 01962 870500. Website: www.hants.gov.uk/museum Fortified residence surrounded by elaborate Civil War earthworks and the subject of a lengthy siege.

Calshot Castle, English Heritage (on a spit of land 2 miles south-east of Fawley, off the B3053). Telephone: 023 8089 2023. One of the earliest of Henry VIII's 'Great Castles', and part of the Solent defences. In the twentieth century the area around the castle was used as a seaplane base.

Fort Brockhurst, English Heritage (off the A32 in Gunner's Way, Elson, on the north side of Gosport). Open for pre-booked parties and on heritage days. Telephone: 01424 775705. One of five substantial, mutually supporting forts forming the Gosport Line of the 1850s, protecting the westward approaches to Portsmouth.

Fort Cumberland, English Heritage (in the Eastney district of Portsmouth, on the estuary approach via Henderson Road, a turning off Eastney Road, or via the Esplanade). Limited opening. Telephone: 01424 775705. The last major bastioned fort to be built in England and one of the first to be provided with casemated guns.

Fort Nelson, Portsdown Hill Road, Fareham, Hampshire PO17 6AN (from Fareham follow A27 eastbound, turn left to climb Portsdown Hill: fort is on left). Telephone: 01329 233734. Website: www.royalarmouries.org An impressive Palmerston fort, now part of the Royal Armouries and containing interesting exhibitions of artillery.

Fort Purbrook, Portsmouth City Council (Portsdown Hill Road, B2177, Cosham, Portsmouth PO6 1BJ). Palmerston fort. Limited opening. Telephone: 023 9232 1223. Website: www.portsmouth.gov.uk

Fort Widley, Portsmouth City Council (Portsdown Hill Road, B2177, Cosham, Portsmouth PO6 1BJ). Palmerston fort. Limited opening. Telephone: 023 9232 1223. Website: www.portsmouth.gov.uk

Hilsea Lines, Portsmouth City Council (bastioned line running across the north of Portsea Island; substantial earthworks and a moat remaining. A self-guided tour leaflet is available from the Hilsea Lines Ranger Service, Bastion 3, Scott Road, Hilsea (telephone: 07958 353152).

Hurst Castle, English Heritage (on a pebble spit south of Keyhaven; best approached by ferry from Keyhaven: telephone 01590 642500 for ferry details). Website: www.hurst-castle.co.uk Beginning as a Henrician artillery fort, its strategic position, projecting into the Needles Passage, has undergone continuous alteration up to and including the Second World War years.

Isle of Wight

Carisbrooke Castle, Isle of Wight PO30 1XY (1¼ miles south-west of Newport). English Heritage. Telephone: 01983 522107. The principal medieval fortress on the island, it was given a bastioned trace in the sixteenth century.

Fort Victoria, near Yarmouth, Isle of Wight PO41 0RR (in Fort Victoria Country Park, 1½ miles west of Yarmouth). Telephone: 01983 823893. Website: www.fortvictoria.co.uk Horseshoe-shaped casemated battery of the 1850s with barracks.

The Needles Old Battery, West Highdown, Totland, Isle of Wight PO39 0JH (spectacularly sited on the westernmost tip of the island). National Trust. Telephone: 01983 754772. Website: www.theneedlesbattery.org.uk Begun in 1862, the battery contains exhibitions on its involvement in both world wars.

Yarmouth Castle, English Heritage (adjacent to the car ferry terminal). Telephone: 01983 760678. Henrician artillery fort with single arrowhead bastion.

Kent

Canterbury city walls. Medieval city walls modified in the late fourteenth century to take firearms.

Deal Castle, English Heritage (south-west of Deal town centre). Telephone: 01304 372762. The most powerful of Henry VIII's artillery forts, it was the major one of the three defending the important Downs anchorage.

Dover Castle, Kent CT16 1HU (on the eastern side of Dover). English Heritage. Telephone: 01304 211067. Medieval castle with later artillery fortifications, the tunnels below the castle being used during the Second World War and the Cold War.

Dymchurch Martello Tower, English Heritage (adjacent to the High Street). Telephone: 01304 211067. Tower number 24 of the seventy-four Martello Towers built between 1805 and 1812.

Fort Amherst, Dock Road, Chatham, Kent ME4 4UB. Telephone: 01634 847747. Website: www.fortamherst.com Complex of fortifications, and the most outstanding Napoleonic era fortification in Britain.

New Tavern Fort (on the eastern side of Gravesend town centre overlooking the Thames). Telephone: 01474 323415. Website: www.gravesham.gov.uk Eighteenth-century fort rebuilt by General Gordon between 1865 and 1874.

Royal Military Canal, National Trust. A 3½ mile (5.6 km) stretch of the canal is owned by the Trust between Appledore and Warehorne.

Upnor Castle, English Heritage (at Upnor on an unclassified road off the A228). Telephone: 01634 718742. Sixteenth-century artillery work built to protect warships moored in the Medway. In 1667 the castle and batteries repulsed a Dutch attack.

Walmer Castle, English Heritage (on the coast south of Walmer on the A258). Telephone: 01304 364288. Henrician fort and from 1708 the residence of the Lord Warden of the Cinque Ports, previous holders of the title being the Duke of Wellington and Winston Churchill.

Western Heights, English Heritage (above Dover town on the west side of the harbour). Telephone: 01223 582774. First fortified in 1779, with substantial further works of the nineteenth century. The spectacular Grand Shaft is open periodically; details of open days can be found on www.dover-western-heights.org

London

Cabinet War Rooms, 1 Clive Steps, King Charles Street, London SW1A 2AQ. Telephone: 020 7930 6961. Website: www.cwr.iwm.org.uk Fortified basement, which in 1940 housed Churchill and his War Cabinet during the Blitz.

HM Tower of London, London EC3N 4AB. Telephone: 0870 756 6060. Website: www.hrp.org.uk A fortified site since Roman and Norman times, it was provided with artillery defences in the late seventeenth century: Legg's Mount and Brass Mount. It was also the home of the Board of Ordnance until its dissolution in the 1850s.

Norfolk

Cow Tower, English Heritage (near Norwich Cathedral). Telephone: 01603 212343. Late-medieval guntower, built as part of the city defences and covering the River Wensum.

Northumberland

Berwick-upon-Tweed town walls, English Heritage. The Elizabethan walls and bastions of the town's defences protect one of the finest surviving fortified towns in Europe. The early-eighteenth-century barracks, bearing the influence of the architect Nicholas Hawksmoor, are also in the care of English Heritage.

Lindisfarne Castle, Holy Island, Berwick-upon-Tweed, Northumberland TD15 2SH. National Trust. Telephone: 01289 389244. Gun platforms and battery constructed in 1542 and maintained into the nineteenth century. Converted into a private residence by Sir Edwin Lutyens in 1902.

Norham Castle, English Heritage (in Norham village, 6½ miles south-west of Berwick on a minor road off the B6470). Telephone: 01289 382329. Medieval castle with gunports and angled towers built in the sixteenth century.

Tynemouth Castle, English Heritage (in the town, near the north pier). Telephone: 0191 257 1090. Medieval castle with traces of sixteenth-century bastioned earthworks and with the magazines and gun positions of a coastal defence battery.

Nottinghamshire

Queen's Sconce, Newark (in Sconce Hills Park, 1 mile south-west of the town centre, off the B6166). Well-preserved example of one of the principal earthworks built during the Civil War siege of Newark.

Somerset

Brean Down Fort, Brean, North Somerset (situated on the seaward point of Brean Down). National Trust. Telephone: 01934 844518. A small Palmerston fort of 1867, with a defensible barracks.

Suffolk

Landguard Fort, English Heritage (1 mile south of Felixstowe, near the docks). Telephone: 07749 695523. Website: www.landguard.com First fortified in the 1540s, provided with its ultimate bastioned trace in the mid eighteenth century, the fort has undergone successive alterations culminating in the granite casemates of the 1870s and a Second World War quick-firing battery.

Surrey

Box Hill Mobilisation Centre, National Trust (exterior only but display boards) (on the summit of Box Hill). One of a number of mobilisation centres along the North Downs, part of the 1890s London Defence Scheme.

Sussex, East

Camber Castle, English Heritage (1 mile walk across fields, off the A529 a mile south of Rye and off the harbour road). Telephone: 01797 223862. Large and elaborate Henrician artillery fort guarding the now-vanished harbour of Camber.

Eastbourne Redoubt, Royal Parade, Eastbourne, East Sussex BN22 7AQ (located by the promenade in the centre of the town). Telephone: 01323 410300. Website: www.eastbournemuseums.co.uk/redoubt One of the three circular redoubts built in the early nineteenth century; it also contains a military museum.

Newhaven Fort, Newhaven, East Sussex BN9 9DS (south of the town, overlooking the River Ouse and harbour). Telephone: 01273 517622. Website: www. newhavenfort.org.uk Fort of the 1860s built to protect the new harbour, with early use of concrete to revet its ditches.

Pevensey Castle, English Heritage (1 mile from Pevensey, reached off the A259). Telephone: 01323 762604. Roman Saxon Shore fort converted into a castle in the Middle Ages, with camouflaged Second World War defence positions built into its walls.

Yorkshire, East

Fort Paull, Battery Road, Paull, near Hull, East Yorkshire HU12 8FP (4 miles to the east of Hull city centre, off the A1033 Hedon road). Telephone: 01482 882655. Website: www.fortpaull.com Victorian coastal battery and submarine mining depot containing a museum.

Scarborough Castle: although of medieval date, it exhibits the damage caused by Parliamentarian gunfire on its keep during the Civil War. In December 1914 the castle was shelled by German warships, one shell passing through the keep.

Yorkshire, North
Helmsley Castle, North Yorkshire YO62 5AB (close to the town centre). English Heritage. Telephone: 01439 770442. Medieval fortress showing the effects of extensive Civil War demolitions.

Scarborough Castle, North Yorkshire YO11 1HY (on Castle Road, east of the town centre). English Heritage. Telephone: 01723 372451. Medieval castle, besieged and damaged in the Civil War, with eighteenth-century master gunner's house. Suffered a naval bombardment in 1914.

CHANNEL ISLANDS
Guernsey
Castle Cornet (on an islet reached by causeway in St Peter Port Harbour). Telephone: 01481 726518. Website: www.museum.guernsey.net Medieval castle with sixteenth-century remodelling for artillery by the military engineers John Rogers and Paul Ive.

Rousse Tower (on the headland on the western side of Ladies Bay in the north of the island). Telephone: 01481 726518. One of a number of Martello Towers and associated batteries built on the island in 1804.

Jersey
Elizabeth Castle (on an island in St Aubin's Bay, reached by a causeway at low tide or by DUKW at high tide). Telephone: 01534 723971. Website: www. jerseyheritagetrust.org Small, irregular, bastioned fort built by Paul Ive in the sixteenth century with later remodelling, including German Second World War work.

Mont Orgueil Castle (above Gorey Harbour in the resort of St Helier). Telephone: 01534 853292. Website: www.jerseyheritagetrust.org Medieval castle, extensively remodelled for artillery in the sixteenth century.

ISLE OF MAN
Derby Fort (at the far end of Langness, near Castletown in the south of the island). Permanently open. A simple Henrician coastal defence artillery fort refortified in the Civil War.

NORTHERN IRELAND
Carrickfergus Castle, County Antrim, Environment and Heritage Service of Northern Ireland (on Marine Highway, Carrickfergus). Originating as a Norman castle, it was converted for artillery defence in the seventeenth century and progressively modified into the nineteenth century.

Londonderry city walls. Seventeenth-century walls with simple bastions and retaining examples of contemporary cannon.

SCOTLAND
Blackness Castle, Historic Scotland (4 miles north-east of Linlithgow, off the A904). Telephone: 01506 834807. Fifteenth-century tower for artillery with sixteenth-century casemated additional artillery defences.

Broughty Castle, Historic Scotland (on the side of the Tay in Broughty Ferry off the A930). Telephone: 01382 436916. A fifteenth-century castle adapted into a coastal defence battery in the 1860s.

Craignethan Castle, Historic Scotland (5½ miles WNW of Lanark, off the A72). Telephone: 01555 860364. Early artillery fortification of c.1530 with tower house and a primitive caponier.

Dumbarton Castle, Historic Scotland (in Dumbarton on the A82). Telephone: 01389 732167. Medieval fortress refortified for artillery in the early eighteenth century, forming part of the defence of the Clyde until the 1850s.

Edinburgh Castle, Historic Scotland. Telephone: 0131 225 9846. Spectacularly sited ancient castle with seventeenth- and eighteenth-century remodelling for artillery.

Fort Charlotte, Historic Scotland (in the centre of Lerwick, Shetland). Telephone: 01856 841815. Five-sided bastioned artillery fort with high and massive walls, burnt by the Dutch in 1673 and rebuilt in 1781.

Fort George, Historic Scotland (6 miles west of Nairn, 11 miles north-east of Inverness, off the A96). Telephone: 01667 460232. Dating from the eighteenth century, it is the mightiest and most extensively preserved artillery fortification remaining in Britain.

Hackness Martello Tower and Battery, Historic Scotland (at the south-east end of Hoy, Orkney). One of a pair of Martello Towers protecting the sound of Longhope.

Inchcolm Abbey, Historic Scotland (on the island of Inchcolm in the Firth of Forth, access by ferry). Telephone: 01383 823332. Part of the inner defences of the Forth, the remains of batteries from both world wars may be seen.

Ravenscraig Castle, Historic Scotland (on the eastern outskirts of Kirkcaldy, off the A955 Dysart road). Dating from the 1460s, it is one of the earliest artillery fortresses in Scotland, consisting of two round towers connected by a cross wall with artillery embrasures.

Ruthven Barracks, Historic Scotland (1 mile from Kingussie, signposted from the A9 and A86 in the centre of Kingussie). Telephone: 01667 460232. Infantry barracks erected in 1719 following the 1715 Jacobite rebellion. Captured and severely damaged by the Jacobite army in 1746.

St Andrews Castle, Historic Scotland (in the town of St Andrews on the A91). Telephone: 01334 477196. Of interest for the survival of the mine and countermine of the siege of 1546–7. There are fragmentary remains of a circular artillery blockhouse from the same century.

Stirling Castle, Historic Scotland. Telephone: 01786 450000. Fortress and royal palace occupying a strategic position at the entry to the Highlands. Much modified, it retains its bastioned and casemated artillery defences.

Tantallon Castle, Historic Scotland (3 miles east of North Berwick, off the A198). Telephone: 01620 892727. A fourteenth-century castle adapted for artillery and with external earthworks dating from the wars of the seventeenth century.

WALES

Laugharne Castle, King Street, Laugharne, Carmarthenshire SA33 4SA. Cadw. Telephone: 01994 427906. Representative of the many medieval Welsh castles that were the subject of a siege in the Civil War.

Pembroke Dock South Western Gun Tower, Pembrokeshire (by the old dock road that runs parallel with the A477 in Pembroke Dock). Telephone: 01646 622246. One of two Victorian guntowers built to defend the Pembroke Dock waterway.

Raglan Castle, Raglan, Monmouthshire NP15 2BT (½ mile north of Raglan, reached via village or off the A40). Cadw. Telephone: 01291 690228. Imposing, late-medieval castle with embrasures for handguns, besieged and slighted in the Civil War.

Further reading

Barrett, John. *A History of the Maritime Forts in the Bristol Channel*. Privately published, 1993.

Beanse, Alec, and Gill, Roger. *The London Mobilisation Centres*. Palmerston Forts Society, 2000.

Burridge, David. *The Dover Turret*. North Kent Books, 1987.

Clements, W. H. *Towers of Strength: Martello Towers Worldwide*. Leo Cooper, 1999.

Clements, W. H. *Defending the North: The Fortifications of Ulster 1796–1956*. Colourpoint, 2003.

Coad, Jonathan. *Dover Castle*. Batsford and English Heritage, 1995.

Cocroft, Wayne. *Dangerous Energy: The Archaeology of Gunpowder and Military Explosives Manufacture*. English Heritage, 2000.

Cocroft, Wayne, and Thomas, Roger. *Cold War: Building for Nuclear Confrontation 1946–1989*. English Heritage, 2003.

Cruden, Stewart. *The Scottish Castle*. Nelson, 1981.

Douet, James. *British Barracks 1600–1914*. The Stationery Office, 2000.

Duffy, Christopher. *Fire and Stone: The Science of Fortress Warfare 1660–1860*. David & Charles, 1996.

Duffy, Christopher. *Siege Warfare: The Fortress in the Early Modern World 1494–1660*. Routledge & Kegan Paul, 1979.

Foot, William. *Beaches, Fields, Streets and Hills: the Anti-Invasion Landscapes of England, 1940*. Council for British Archaeology, 2006.

Gaunt, Peter. *A Nation under Siege: The Civil War in Wales 1642–48*. HMSO, 1991.

Goodwin, John. *The Military Defence of West Sussex*. Middleton Press, 1985.

Harrington, Peter. *English Civil War Fortifications 1642–51*. Osprey, 2003.

Hogg, Ian. *Coast Defences of England and Wales 1856–1956*. David & Charles, 1974.

Hughes, Quentin. *Military Architecture*. Oxbow, 1974.

Keightly, Charles, and Chèze-Brown, Peter. *Strongholds of the Realm*. Book Club Associates, 1979.

Kent, Peter. *Fortifications of East Anglia*. Terence Dalton, 1988.

Kinross, John. *The Palmerston Forts of the South West: Why Were They Built?* Privately published, 1988.

Lewis, Major J. F. *Permanent Fortification for English Engineers*. First published 1890; reprinted 2005 by D. G. & P. Military Publishers, Doncaster, Yorkshire.

Longmate, Norman. *Island Fortress: The Defence of Great Britain 1603–1945*. Grafton, 1993.

Lowry, Bernard. *British Home Defences 1940–45*. Osprey, 2004.

McCamley, N. J. *Secret Underground Cities*. Leo Cooper, 1998.

Mitchell, Garry. *Hilsea Lines and Portsbridge*. Privately published, 1988.

Moore, David. *A Handbook of Military Terms*. The Palmerston Forts Society, 1993.

Osborne, Mike. *Defending Britain: Twentieth-Century Military Structures in the Landscape*. Tempus Publishing, 2004.

Osborne, Mike. *Sieges and Fortifications of the Civil Wars in Britain*. Partizan Press, 2004.

Partridge, Colin, and Davenport, Trevor. *The Fortifications of Alderney*. Alderney Publishers, 1993.

Patterson, Professor A. Temple. *'Palmerston's Folly'. The Portsdown and Spithead Forts: The Portsmouth Papers No.3*. Portsmouth City Council, 1974.

Pye, Andrew, and Woodward, Freddy. *The Historic Defences of Plymouth*. Cornwall County Council, 1996.

Saunders, Andrew. *Fortress Britain*. Oxbow Books, 1989.

Saunders, Andrew. *Fortress Builder: Bernard de Gomme, Charles II's Military Engineer*. University of Exeter Press, 2004.

Saunders, Andrew *et al. Guns across the Severn: The Victorian Fortifications of Glamorgan*. Royal Commission on the Ancient and Historical Monuments of Wales, 2001.

Smith, V. T. C. *Defending London's River: The Story of the Thames Fortifications*. North Kent Books, 1985.

Smith, V. T. C. *Front Line Kent*. Kent County Council, 2001.

Tabraham, Christopher. *Scottish Castles and Fortifications*. Historic Scotland, 1986.

Van der Bijl, Nicholas. *Brean Down Fort*. Hawk Editions, 2000.

Wiggins, Kenneth. *Siege Mines and Underground Warfare*. Shire Publications, 2003.

Woodward, F. W. *Plymouth's Defences: A Short History*. Privately published, 1990.

Woodward, Freddy. *Forts or Follies? A History of Plymouth's Palmerston Forts*. Halsgrove, 1998.

JOURNALS AND SOCIETIES

In addition to the publications listed there are excellent guides to individual fortifications in the care of the major heritage bodies and published by them.

Castle Studies Group: Membership Secretary, David Bartlett, 4 Cotley Place, Heytesbury, Warminster, Wiltshire BA12 0HT. Website: www.castlestudiesgroup. org.uk Email: membership@castlestudiesgroup.org.uk

The Fortress Study Group, 6 Lanark Place, London W9 1BS. Website: www.fsgfort.com Publishes a thrice yearly magazine called *Casemate* and an annual journal, *Fort*.

The Palmerston Forts Society, Fort Nelson, Portsdown Hill Road, Fareham, Hampshire PO17 6AN. Website: www.palmerstonforts.org.uk Publishes the magazine *Redan*.

The UK Fortifications Club/Pillbox Study Group, 3 Chelwood Drive, Taunton, Somerset TA1 4JA. Website: www.pillbox-study-group.org.uk Publishes a magazine, *Loopholes/Aldis*.

Martello Tower, Felixstowe, Suffolk: this is the original door, still retaining its locking mechanism. Above it is a smoke vent. Note the depth of the wall.

Index

Page numbers in italic refer to illustrations.